I WOKE UP TO WIN

I WOKE UP TO
WIN

A DAY-BY-DAY PLAYBOOK FOR REIGNING,
RULING AND WINNING IN LIFE

JOE N. UNION

FOREWORD BY SCOTT DAVENPORT, PH.D.

Ink City
PRESS

Library of Congress Cataloging-in-Publication Data
Union, Joe N. 1984 –

I Woke Up to Win; A Day-by-day Playbook for Reigning, Ruling, and Winning in Life by Joe N. Union

ISBN: 978-0-9973519-8-9 H
       978-0-9973519-9-6 P
       978-0-6928395-4-6 E

Includes bibliographical references and index
1. Christian Living   2. Inspirational I. Title

First Edition
Printed in the United States of America
2017944404

For bookings and engagements
www.iwokeup2win.com

Rights for publishing this work outside the United States of America or in non-English languages are administered by Ink City Press.

I Woke Up to Win

Is not just a phrase or saying;
It's a conviction.
It is who I am, it is who you are, and it is who we are.
Winning is not just what we do;
It is what we were born to do,
It is the reason why we are here.
It is our purpose, it is our destiny,
It is our calling, it is the reason we were created,
And If We Wake Up, We've Won.

For Tavara

ACKNOWLEDGEMENTS

———

To my lovely wife, Tavara Union, my queen and a faithful friend indeed. You have always been by my side. You entrusted me with your dreams, goals, aspirations, and future, to lead the way that God has directed. You believe that I seek God's counsel for our well-being, and you trust me for your safety and security. You believe in me to do what God has called me to do. There were times when you sacrificed to take care of the things we needed and you never complained. You are a strong, wise woman of God and there is no one like you. There is no one with whom I would rather be on this journey sharing my life. Thank you for being a wonderful wife and my best friend.

To my loving parents, Joe and Diana Union, thank you for being vessels of life and for being an instrument of God's grace, favor, and love. Thank you for instilling in my sisters and me values and morals, which are the finer things in life that money cannot buy. They help when no one is around, when there is nowhere to run, and no one to call.

You gave us the real recipe to life, and not only did you tell us, but you also showed us how to win. To my mother, thank you for being loving. Thank you for being strong. Thank you for being a mighty woman of God. To my father, thank you for showing me what a modern-day man after God's own heart looks like.

You were not one to just talk about love, you showed it. You are a man of wisdom and many sayings. Two of my favorites are, "Do what you can while you can," and "Time takes care of most things." I thank you both for the authentic love and kindness that you show toward our family and the community.

To my caring sisters, Andrea and JoQuita, thank you for being the thread and needle hemming me in on both sides, and keeping me from completely going astray. To my nieces, Aunjane, Autumn, and Amber, Uncle loves you. Your futures are full of blessings.

To my brother, Eric Edmonds, a great friend, a true visionary, a gentleman, and a scholar, prolific writer and international consultant. I'm so proud of your success in business. As an ambassador, you've handled affairs well. You're an amazing son, brother, father, husband, and most importantly a God-fearing man. Thank you for being a great brother, for your kind words of wisdom, always offering genuine business advice and powerful key points to advance in life. You are the friend who enjoys seeing others succeed, offering ideas and ingenuity without taking any credit. What a gem. I am honored to call you my brother.

I have been most fortunate to have had a dynamic teacher and counselor, Dr. Scott Davenport as a mentor. It is his invaluable insights through God's unchanging and unfailing word that has inspired a young man like myself.

To Dr. Remus E. Wright and Mia K. Wright, thank you for investing a great deal of sound biblical principles through the years, all of which has become the foundation for my own life. You have helped mold my faith in Christ in countless ways, and for all that, I am forever grateful.

I thank Walter August Jr. and Ruby August, for an

authenticity in character that pierces yet with a grace that up-
lifts at every turn. You have been an honorable man of God,
wisdom and grace, and I sincerely appreciate your love and
support.

Thank you to Willie Lee Smalls, a dear brother whose model of
friendship and encouragement have meant the world to me. Thank
you for sharing your words of wisdom through the paths you have
travelled. It is the quality of the words you share that continues to
empower young men and women to pursue their passions.

Thank you Chuck Gremillion for being a dynamic busi-
ness owner and friend. Your genuineness and generosity are
well received and you have impacted and help shape many
lives. To Steve Pontiff, thank you for lending me your ear as
an entrepreneur and a business thinker. My gratitude to James
Cunningham, Phillip, Terrence and Sam Troupe, Cronelius
Williams, Darin and Tyra Jones, Jontai Perry, Jacques Irby,
Corneshia Williams, Britni Nelson-Williams, Lonell Williams,
Dietrich Hall, Claudia Horton, Lakesha Yancey, Terrence Clark,
John Jeans, and all my family who have been incredibly instru-
mental in one way or the other to the person I would become.
My Grandmother Granny Hall, Mom Theresa Jernigan and Big
Momma Margaret Bell, it is with your prayers that our genera-
tion will carry on our lives with, thank you a great deal.

Jamilah Robinson, I appreciate all of your dedication and
commitment to turn this manuscript into what it became. I am
truly grateful.

My special gratitude also to the brilliant Jason Hooey, for
enduring the laborious task of creative excellence. You have
been a great friend, and I am forever grateful for your coming
along with me on this journey.

For the team at Ink City Press and Atlantic Media Group, it has indeed been a privilege to work with you, and thank you for the genuine care and grace you bring to a project.

This journey has been indeed gratifying, and I am immensely grateful for God's abundant grace to have seen me through it all.

CONTENTS

———

FOREWORD

––––––

I Woke Up to Win is a blueprint for winning in life. Winning is more about attitude than skills, talents and abilities. A skill, talent or ability can take you through seasons of life, but a healthy attitude will take you through life victoriously with all of its challenges.

We all have the ability to develop healthy attitudes. Our attitude is our way of thinking. The onset begins in early childhood. We have an experience. We evaluate and interpret the experience, and draw a conclusion. That conclusion becomes our attitude.

Our attitude and way of thinking determine how we feel, behave or perform in any situation. Developing a right attitude is a must to be able to consistently win in the game of life. Since our attitude is our thought-life and our thought-life determines our behavior, we must always strive to maintain a right attitude. In order to do this, we must become aware of where our habits come from.

We have a conscious and subconscious mind. Our habits come from our subconscious and they control us whether we want them to or not. In order to maintain a continual awareness of our thoughts, we must be in touch with our feelings and emotions. Since our emotions come from what we think and our habitual behavior is subconscious, we have to stay in touch with our emotional state. When we feel a certain way it is because we are thinking a certain way. Consequently, we will act accordingly.

When we can identify our feelings and emotions we can trace them to the thoughts that are producing them. Once we are aware of the thoughts, we then have the ability to reprogram our minds by downloading new ones. When our thoughts change, our feelings and emotions change, and behavioral change is automatic.

In *I Woke Up to Win*, Joe Union uses the great American pastime of football to teach us how to develop and use this process. Read, hear, learn and change. Victory and success will be yours.

—Scott Davenport, Ph.D.

INTRODUCTION

———

Welcome to the Gridiron.

I spent the early years of my life listening to people say "Life is not a game," "You must take life seriously," and "Don't play around." As I grew up and started to encounter more responsibilities, I was quickly comforted by life's rushing force called adulthood that would have me stand on my own two feet. In fact, let's look at life through the lens of a game for a moment, "in the game of life. I was too young to understand that much of what I was about to endure in my adolescent life and as a young adult would be largely influenced by my own actions and attitudes. If life was indeed a game, I wished someone had informed me that very soon I would be walking onto the field and be at the center stage in my own life, taking my first step.

As I was growing up, American football had become the new national pastime in the United States and Canada. Every Sunday was packed with passionate conversations about who played, who won, and most importantly, why those teams won. As fans of the game watching it from the comfort of our homes on television, we all seemed to know exactly what the players should be doing on the field. If there was a possibility of trading places, we would be just as puzzled. Winning takes work.

Winning takes strategy and an incredible amount of readiness. It is easy to lose sight of the fact that the team who emerges as a winner had to work the entire week, and what we see on Sunday is only manifestation of what was done behind the scenes.

Such is life. God has given each of us an amazing gift of today. We have an opportunity to live every day with a victorious outlook, if we understand our position on life's field, and understand exactly what the next moment requires of us. Football is a microcosm of life. In *I Woke Up To Win*, there are the connections between our lives as we all live them, and the amazing puzzles and lessons in a football game, and the grace God gives us every step along the way to live out our dreams. The concept of the ultimate football game is taken from an offensive point of view. You are the quarterback who manages game play and directs the team down the field. How will you play the four quarters that have been given to you?

Every day that God allows us the opportunity to see should be embraced with enthusiasm, urgency, and intensity of every thought. Each day, we are all blessed with 1,440 minutes, and our objective is to reach the end zone, obtaining points that lead to victory. Strive to score a touchdown every day, one moment at a time. God is gracious and merciful to give us the ball of dreams, talent, goals, drive, courage, passion, and purpose. Our challenge is to take the ball of opportunity and march it down the field of life in order to score points, get touchdowns, and win.

We all carry a desire to win, and accomplish the goals we set for ourselves. Excellence and success are not always tangible, but if at the end of the day, we can look ourselves in the mirror and know that we have given our best effort, we are on our way to winning. If we are able to tap into what God has destined for us, use the playbook and the tremendous training opportunities to execute every day, we will win. If we find in ourselves the will to win, and are patient enough to take one play at a time, giving it our best effort, we will win.

Spiritual Football – A Global Game
The game is played IN the world, ON the field of life, AT the stadium of Christ in front of a sold-out crowd.

The Field of Life
Your Profession
We, as humans, must understand that we are to be alert and aware, that we are to retain knowledge to equip ourselves to play this supernatural football game.

The Offense
You— The Quarterback
God— The Head Coach
Jesus— The Offensive Coordinator
Holy Spirit— The Quarterback Coach
Team— The Fruit of the Spirit
Cheerleaders— Spouse, Family, Friends
Angels— Referees
The Ball—Dreams, Visions, and Goals

The Defense
Devil — Head Coach
Demons— Principalities and Rulers of Darkness
Acts of the Flesh

All honor, power, praise, and glory goes to my Heavenly Father. He has expressed his love to us through his son, Yeshua, the Christ, and has given us his Holy Spirit to dwell inside of us to be the light that shines in our hearts. God is my inspiration for writing this book.

He is the reason that we wake up — that in itself is a win — to a new day of opportunities to impact our fellow neighbors and communities, throughout cities and states, fulfilling His will in the world.

CHAPTER ONE

SCOUTED
WE ARE GOD'S STORY

Play Call: Jeremiah 1:5

"Before I formed you in the womb I knew you, before you were born I set you apart; I appointed you as a prophet to the nations."

What if someone sits in the crowd watching our every move and every step to see us at our best? What if someone patiently evaluates every single breath we breathe to make sure that we are th right height, the right size, and even the right temperament? A scout does just that, through the pouring rain and the scorching sun, in search for someone who would belong to a team. That is his assignment, and he is on a mission.

A player knows the scout in the stands may be his only chance of making it onto a professional team. If the scout looks on him favorably, maybe the owners and coaches will too. Pleasing the scout becomes just as crucial as every jump and step. The player knows this, and he desperately wants to earn a favorable rating, so that even when he is worn, tired and cannot push any further, he tries even harder. But what if after all that, the scout still finds the player unworthy?

What if we knew we were selected even before the scout took his seat in the bleachers? What if even before we had the ability to take a step, someone had run ahead of us and labelled us worthy?

Worthy is how God sees you and me. Even before we could choose what team to be a part of, He knew what would be best for you and me, and marked us worthy. He watches our every move knowing every potential and pitfall in our life, but our scouting grade doesn't change. Somehow God knows that even after all the favorable grade, He will need to sacrifice a great deal to have us in His team, but that doesn't deter Him.

A professional team will spend an enormous amount of effort and money to evaluate potential. They cannot possibly know what they are getting in a player, so they are uneasy. They take all the precautions. That is why the scout sits in the rain and sun to find out all he can. Yet there is a scout who knows every flaw and knows the risk that comes from having us in His team, but He still is choosing to give us a high grade. He considers us worthy.

It is God's love that chose us even when we were yet to be formed in our mother's wombs, long before the blood began to flow through our veins. Our potential is mystery to us, but certainly not to Him. There are no "intangibles" and unanswered questions that will cause God to pause in His evaluation of you and me. The scout is in love with us, and He so desperately wants you and me, just as we are. One thing the scout is confident of is what He could make of us— a perfect fit for His team. There is nothing we can do in our own strength to deserve this favor. Unlike the football player, whose dream is to walk across the bright lights on a stage on draft day, there is nothing we could possibly do to earn that spotlight and be drafted by God. He knew you and me long before we had an option of subjecting our free will into His hands, and He decided then that we were worth the price. Someday, we would be worth His selection.

As a kid in my neighborhood, I remember watching the older boys playing recreational sports. They spent much of their afternoons playing football. It was one of their favorites as well as mine but all the young people always had to watch the bigger fellas play first. We saw them having fun and we wanted more than anything to get on the field too. But to them, we were not qualified. We were neither tall enough, strong enough nor fast enough to be on their teams. We had to plead our case, but it seems nothing we could say made a difference. We did not have anyone to advocate on our behalf.

All we could do was to stand on the sidelines as we watched them slam each other to the ground with all their might. We hoped and wished to play with them. The teams were set; they couldn't add any one of us. Sure, we had potential, and had passion, but all that still wasn't enough to let them even consider adding any one of us. We wished they had seen us playing on any other occasion, and seen who we could become. Maybe we would have had our chance on the field, if we had someone who could imagine who we could become.

BUT SOMETHING HAPPENED!

Far, far away there was a game that had already been played and won (Revelation 12:7-11). The two opponents faced each other. It was a head-to-head match featuring Satan, the ruler of this world versus God, Creator of Heaven and Earth. This was an uneven match-up; one could tell before kick-off that this game would not even be close. The coaches had different viewpoints and philosophies; one taught winning in love while the other's strategy centered on winning in rage. Satan's team had an outward beauty like no other.

They were covered in every precious stone this world offered: sardius, topaz, diamonds, beryl, onyx, jasper, sapphire, turquoise, and emeralds with gold (Ezekiel 28: 12-15).

This corrupted coach had the appearance of strength but no power. His mindset and attitude were reckless and dangerous, full of striving, anger, hatred, envy, deceit and lies. Satan forcefully recruited his starting lineup, to challenge the other team and its players, and they lost (Revelation 12:4). Due to their defeat, they were eliminated from life's playoffs. Satan's defeat placed us midfield of a spiritual football game (Revelation 12:7-11).

This is the league that we are fighting our way onto a field to play in. Our strength alone cannot guarantee us a victory. The opponents understand very well that there is one team against which it can never win, and their goal is to yank away any possibility of getting on God's team.

To make it into a professional football league, a person would have to be an elite athlete, demonstrate top speed, and show awareness. Beyond the mental requirements, they would need to have the stature, physique and other superior talents. The physical traits would take the draft pick pretty far, and it's considered a bonus if you possess the knowledge of the sport. The prospective player's Intelligent Quotient (IQ) is what the scout imagines would help a player to stand out among millions of equally skilled athletes in the world.

The scouts busily do their due diligence, and do so with a set of expectations which they believe defines the person. We are all blessed with some type of special skill, talent, or gift that God provided. There are many men and women that could easily qualify for the professional league but they simply have not believed that they could. They have not taken the time or applied themselves, and so have missed opportunities and given up. There are many that can play but not all make it. Looking forward to the opportunity to be drafted is special. It's a privilege to be able to do the thing you were created to do, on a major platform, and also to be compensated for doing so.

Before a football player is drafted, he goes through a series of on-the-field drills to show his physical abilities and skills. For the professional league, this has become the highly anticipated Scouting Combines. It is the dedicated time and place where all the scouts get an up-close look at potential candidates they are considering drafting for their teams. Scouts are not just merely assessing an athlete's physical abilities, but are also looking for what they consider a "complete package." They are evaluating the player for a specific purpose, and to fulfil a mission.

There are three major areas that are considered when a player goes through the scouting combines: An athlete is observed and scouted as the person, the performer and the player.

The Person

The candidate as the person is being assessed for the kind of character and behavior he displays outside the game. Does he have any major off-the-field issues? Does he stay out of trouble?

The Performer

The candidate as an athlete is scouted at the combines based on his performance, drills and routines to judge his, endurance, power, skills and physical abilities.

The Player

The candidate as a player is assessed on how well he works with others. Coaches, general managers, and owners depend on college game film to determine a player's raw talent and work ethic. They assess the chemistry and bond with his former teammates and forecast how good a fit he will be for the team.

The combines present an opportunity that only comes once in a year and you must be prepared. We ought not think that we have all the time in the world to make our dreams happen; we must be ready to win.

Truth is, there are plenty of talented people, athletes, singers, actresses and actors in this world, but what sets you apart is God's favor.

Each of us would have to ask ourselves the question, that if someone was to scout us and review our life's resumé, what would they see? What would they say? Would they see you and me as the perfect team player? Would they see you and me as a person willing to learn and grow? Would they see you and me as being quick to help, and excited to develop into the person they imagine we could become?

It is a joy to know that God drafted us in spite of our physical attributes — our physique, shape, size, color, intellect, background or financial status. None of these characteristics mattered because He had His eye on us from the beginning.

We are all MVPs in the eyes of our Father; prized possessions and masterfully crafted. We just have to be coached up to the level for which we were created.

Players are not only expected to play football, but to be consistent, versatile and well rounded. They are expected to have the composure for pre- and post-game interviews, answering tough questions. These candidates are asked questions that really do not have an impact on the player's athletic skills and abilities. These questions are a test to ensure that the candidates are well prepared off the field, as well as on the field, because mental pressure could possibly impact a player during the game.

Mental preparation is just as important because opponents will try things to get a player off his game, attempting to make him irrelevant. In order to combat this situation, coaches must know how to manage their players, in the same manner that the Lord knows how to deal with us.

But the perfect scout — our Heavenly Father — looks across the field, and sees the opposing team just as eager to get us on their side. He knows very well that we are full of passion and deep in our hearts will be a willingness to submit our will into His hands. He calls each one of us by our names. He whispers to our hearts to get ready to get on the field and trust Him to lead us every step along the way. He had seen us before the foundations of the earth and is willing to pay any price to have us. The strange part becomes that our shortcomings are as glaring as they can be, yet He loves us too much to allow us to slip through His fingers.

God already made His decision on us. Our handicaps and shortcomings are not enough of a blemish to make Him change His mind. The scout already decided on you and me. He has already chosen you and me for His highest purpose, and called us worthy.

CHAPTER TWO

DRAFTED

On Purpose for a Purpose

Play Call: Ephesians 1:4

"For he chose us in him before the creation of the world to be holy and blameless in his sight. In love."

As a young man carries a dream of someday being drafted into the professional football league, he imagines being in a spotlight with millions of people watching and celebrating his every step. For every passion that he has nurtured up until this moment, every one of life's decisions, every practice and habit have led him to this crossroad.

Yet, one thing he knows for sure is that there are only a few slots on each team. They are the few desired spots that millions of people just like him yearn for. So when the young man sits back, he ponders over what life will hold at the two extreme ends of the pendulum.

He could end up with a football team and see his dream

come alive. In that same instant, he could see his dream of being in the league shattered and denied when everything he has worked so hard for fails to earn him one of the coveted slots on a team.

The draft is when individuals who are considered the best in their respective positions on a football field are selected to be a part of a new team. They get a new identity.

The best part of life is the fact that once we wake up every day to see a new sun, and our lungs get a chance to breathe, we have indeed been selected for a slot. Every morning we are fortunate to be alive is a draft day. Every day is game-day, and being alive is compelling evidence enough that our God-given assignments on this earth will get to go on for at least another day. Unlike the young man who prepares eagerly, with his fate left in the hands of other people who have their own expectations and ambitions, we go through life's draft under the watchful eye of a Heavenly Father. He loves us so much that He extends His mercies towards us every day. Even when we are the least worthy of His love, it is His unfailing grace that continually keeps us in His arms. It keeps us in bounds.

We breathe another day, not by accident, but because the God who created all of the heavens and the earth chose us to live. The intriguing thought becomes that He could have chosen anybody, anywhere, and for such a time as this. He chose you and me. We were drafted to live; drafted to a team where our assignment is to plough through the day the very best way we know how and to win with every *possession*.

We are drafted on purpose, and drafted for a purpose. In the case of the football game, whenever we observe the potential player standing in limbo on draft day, we see how all the confidence he has left in him lies in what he has committed himself to, for weeks and months and years. He finds assurance in the fact that all of the rigorous trainings and the endless efforts have brought him to the brink of this opportunity.

Athletes devote themselves to an extraordinary amount of drills and regimens to help them become faster, stronger and bigger. Their whole ambition is to see themselves as the gladiators in centuries past who took pride in their impressive strength and physique. Draft day puts their hopes on full display. Their hope is in the hands of someone they cannot influence.

Everything in a person's life worth measuring is measured. Every mistake and every missed opportunity is scrutinized. Ultimately the goal is to be sure even the seemingly minor inefficiencies and undesirable tendencies don't become one's Achilles heel in the next phase of life. Hard work brought the athlete to this point, but grace brings him to the draft day of life.

God's unrelenting grace is one that we cannot buy nor work for. It is a grace that is found only through Jesus Christ who loved us so much that he looked down at a world with billions of people, and chose us. We are chosen for such a time as this. We have been drafted.

We cannot select ourselves onto the team. Because we have absolutely no control over anything in our physical being when we close our eyes at night to sleep, it is impossible to take credit for the morning that comes after. Unlike the draft day for a football player where he can count on his own ability, there is probably nothing as humbling as the thought that our ability cannot vouch for us. If we were to be judged by how we performed the day before, and the purity of our lives became the prerequisite for waking up to see another sunrise, none of us would make it. None of us would have even been considered.

Most of us have never taken a moment to think twice about why we lived to see another morning. We do not realize how important we are to God's game plan, or how He intends on working through us for His glory. This is how we can live in the confidence that being alive is a great testament that God's plan for our lives is unfinished. In fact, it has only begun. We have been drafted with a hope. We have been drafted with a plan and for a purpose.

Just as in football, draft day comes along with a host of expectations, but the biggest is the hope that the person the team ultimately selects will be willing to strive to excel. The player's work is to give the team owners who have taken a chance on him all the reasons why his selection has not been a mistake.

God the Father gave up his first-round draft pick, Jesus Christ, to us. He did this in the final round that we will reign, rule and win. It was, and still is, God's desire that we hit the field with purpose, power and passion.

DRAFT DAY

God the Father, God the Son, and God the Holy Spirit drafted you and me. His one desire was to make man in His own image, and after His likeness. He intended that we "have dominion over the fish of the sea, and over the fowl of the air, and over the cattle, and over all the earth." A God who loved us even before we had anything to offer had you and me in mind in the draft room.

It was a perfect team – the Holy Trinity – that saw how great you and I would become. They saw how intelligent we would be, even in the face of our less than intelligent decisions. They saw how strong we were, even when we couldn't muster the courage to take even the first step. The day you and I were born, we were drafted.

The amazing truth is that we came into this life with the ball of hope, success, dreams, goals and visions. You and I are the "opportunity." We have been masterfully and fearfully formed in God's own image, and there is nothing else out there we should be looking for. There is no greater team, and no better opportunity worth trading for what God has chosen us to do. When God drafted you and me into this *game of life*, He weaved His purpose and promise into the very fabric of our inner being. Our confidence rests in the fact that He equipped us with everything we need to be the players He created us to be. We have to go all out and play hard at full speed. The challenge is ours to not allow the opponent of life to slow us down with distractions. There will always be a myriad of situations and circumstances that will happen to all of us, but through it all, we can rest knowing that we have already won.

We were dropped into this stadium called Planet Earth, with a mandate to work out our win in the world. You and I are here to dominate, to reign, to rule and to win (Genesis 1:26-31).

We were created to defeat the enemy, and formed to conquer our opponent. Nothing in us is inferior. There is nothing that can stop us, as we are built and equipped by Almighty God to win in this game of life. We have the character of a true winner and the heart of a conqueror. Winning is in our genes. Winning is in our DNA; it is what we are made of.

One thing I have found out through the years is that there are two things that all humans have in common. The first is the yearning to wake up and the other is to win. The fact remains, however, that waking up is the only requirement to staying on the field.

The football game is designed with the primary position being a quarterback. His work is incredibly integral to the success of the team, because it is in his hands that the ball remains at the critical decision-making moment. The coaches go to great lengths to make sure the quarterback is equipped, confident and well-prepared to take on the task at hand.

You and I are the quarterbacks of our lives and are responsible for carrying our team up the field every day. Our team is our inheritance that God has blessed us with. He knows we cannot do it alone, and loved us enough to surround us with an awesome team. We get to stand shoulder to shoulder with a tremendous team — the fruit of the Spirit. The starting lineup — from love, joy, peace, patience, kindness, goodness, faithfulness, gentleness, to self-control —plays a critical part in our victory (Galatians 5:22-23). This will assist you getting the ball up the field.

In football, the ball is very important to all the players regardless of their positions on the field. The offense needs the ball, just as much as the defense demands it. In this spiritual game, the ball represents our dreams and goals. The ball is our vision, talents and gifts. God has given us the ball of hope, purpose and promise.

There will always be the offensive side of the ball, which is the opportunity to advance in the fullness of what God has intended for us. The objective of the game is to ultimately win and every waking moment is our pursuit of a Heavenly target. There is a divine game plan that maps out our victory. Every day that

God allows us to wake up is a win. The ball of hope and promise is kicked off to our own end zone with the expectation that we will run with vigor, knowing that there is a grace that will carry us when our strength alone cannot take us any further. We have a hope and a future. Just like in football we have the option to run and explore the field in the face of opposition. It will be on our shoulders to determine whether it is worth pursuing extra yards or give up where we stand.

God is calling you and me to trust his guidance to keep moving. Advance the ball with every stride. Forward progress through prayer and a submission to the will of Almighty God is what the team counts on us to do. On the football field, a player will yield by kneeling in the end zone, having made the decision to start on the twenty-five-yard line. We have to keep moving.

We are all blessed to have a choice on how and where to start. There is God's unfailing grace that enables you and me to use our God-given talents to make the right call. My encouragement is that we will know that we were drafted as a champion to bring glory to God through how we live, and how we demonstrate His will in our lives. The world is our field to work out our win that was ordained from the beginning of time.

We were designed to be on the field; we would not have been born if we hadn't been selected by God to play the game of life. He intends for us to be victorious. We were drafted for a reason. There exists a purpose God had us in mind before the foundations of this earth. On the draft day, God drafted us knowing that we were capable of greatness because He installed it into the core of our being. God planted a seed of greatness in our hearts and once we discover the seed — which is faith in Christ —we have unlocked the game plan for our win. The enemy will expend all his energy to use self-inflicted conflict within us to taint the seed of success. The enemy hope is to derail you and me by manipulating us into misusing our gifts. Even worse, abandoning our God-given gifts. For the seed that God has planted in us to blossom, it is incredibly important that we continuously protect our soil against a defense that is bent on planting flags of doubt on every play.

As children of the most-high God we should be excited that a winning coach, who has never lost, drafted us on a winning team. We ought to be excited for the opportunity to play in the great arena of life. What we know for sure is that there are unknown numbers of people not yet born, that have not yet been drafted into the game of life, but our heavenly coach selected us to suit up and make a difference. We are the testimony.

Being drafted is an honor and a privilege to get on the field and play in front of the adoring fans, cheering friends, and loving family. Our being drafted is like that moment which every football player works hard for all of his life. Our draft becomes the culmination of all the long nights and early mornings making necessary sacrifices in hopes that one day our names will be called to walk across that stage. There the light will be bright, and there will be crowds of witnesses to see a player put on the team's cap and to hold up his jerseys with his name inscribed on it.

Even when we stood so far apart because of who we have been, our Heavenly father runs towards you and me with His embrace. We learn that even when our sins were like scarlet, God's grace turned them white as snow.

ROOKIE YEAR

After being drafted into the family of Christ, you and I may not know what to do next. It will not be obvious which way to go. For many of us, there will be many questions to which we will desperately seek answers. Like the player that has been selected to be a part of a perfect team, we will wonder what our role is on God's team. Are we a starter or have we been drafted to sit on the bench and observe? We will live with our own questions of what we ought to be doing to fit in on a new team.

In our minds, like most rookies that enter a football league, we will have to know that we have something worthy to offer and contribute in a big way. Like the rookie in a football game that spends every moment focused on the fact that he indeed has something to prove, he will be immensely thankful to the coaching staff for believing in him enough to have drafted him. As rookies on God's team, you and I live with the thought that now is the time to show our coaches what we were drafted to do. The expectation and high hopes are apparent. But the great news is, unlike the football league, being drafted to God's team means we immediately get onto the field to play. God knew that we would be equipped for the purpose to which He has called us, and there will be no time needed to sit back and watch others live their lives before we begin to live ours.

We will not have to worry about measuring up to anyone's expectations because the Coach who drafted you and me knew exactly what we were made of when He selected us at a hefty price. God drafted you and me knowing that we would be a work in progress, but just as clay finds its value in the master's hand and on the potter's wheel, God wants us to get acclimated into to His system, after which the rest will fall into place. He knows that you and I will pick up and learn all the techniques that will transform us from rookies into a people on a journey toward becoming a celebrated quarterback. God knows that we will have to endure the process that peels away the immature tendencies, so that ultimately He can mold us in the way He has set for us.

On His team, our old self is stripped away one day at a time, because what the Almighty God is counting on is to see us adjust and adapt into the professionals that we can become. God will search us, show us, and shape us into the person He wants us to be. Our responsibility is to plug into His offensive system, follow His game plan and listen to the Quarterback Coach, the Holy Spirit. There will be many times when as new believers we will be unsure of how to be, how to act, and even what to say. We want to be authentic but want to fit into our new team. We do all this while fighting to ward off our old habits, and ways we have lived.

Fortunately, we can embrace our new team. Drafted onto a new team will require you and me to spend time listening, learning, studying, observing, and implementing. Listening closely to the coaching staff is very vital to our own growth. We will have to grow to great heights, and there will be nothing more crucial than the quiet moments that we deeply spend one-on-one, listening to the Quarterbacks Coach, the Holy Spirit.

Our being a draft pick was not an accident. There is a God who predestined you and me to play this game, and to do so on His team. It is my prayer that we do not take being our drafted for granted. But now that we are drafted, the work begins.

CHAPTER THREE

TRAINING CAMP

Search Me, Show Me, Shape Me,

Play Call: 2 Timothy 2:15

"Study to show thyself approved unto God, a workman who needeth not to be ashamed, rightly dividing the word of truth."

Know that once you have been drafted, saved or born again, it is the beginning of a journey. Now the real work begins. The task ahead is for you and me to get ready to play at a high level, at full speed, and with exuberance every day on every play.

We have been scouted by God, and drafted onto his team by waking up on a new day. We have to be prepared to run Christ's offense that is bound to confuse Satan's defense, and win the ultimate game. Our God has chosen you and me for our victory to be His glory, but the work will be ours to execute.

SUIT-UP

I recall many special mornings from when I worked at Houston's Reliant Stadium, a few years ago. It was home to the Houston Texans organization. On the days where a game was scheduled, I would arrive early in the morning, around 7:00 a.m. That was several hours before the game, and before the fans showed up in the stands. The stadium's atmosphere was incredibly different from what it would become just a few hours into the afternoon. It was quiet and empty. Then, slowly, the fans trickled in, row after row. Then the spot lights came on, and the players ran out onto the field. The crowd cheered and the game was set to begin.

There are a lot of intricate details that are planned days in advance, all for a game that lasts 60 minutes. Just as the workers prepare for the game, the players get ready many hours before they hear the sound of the adoring fans.

It is the same as when an event planner is planning a party. There are tasks that must be done in order for the event to run smoothly. When the guests arrive, they are amazed, but certainly without knowing exactly what took place behind the scenes for the event to become a marvelous one. Every event that we celebrate — from Broadway musicals, ballroom dances, weddings and banquets, to birthday parties— all take planning, training, and preparation in order to execute an unforgettable experience.

The same is true for athletes. I was fortunate on those mornings to walk around the stadium and see an athlete running on the sides of the field hours before anyone would have expected him to do so. Fans see them on the field scoring points and making fascinating plays, but no one sees the hard work they dedicate themselves to away from the field.

Preparation is lonely. There are no cheering fans holding cute signs to inspire the athlete to keep going. It is uneventful. Preparation away from the bright lights may seem arduous and time consuming, but the athlete understands the value of every step. The most strenuous of exercises are all building him up for an opposition he will face when the lights are on. He knows this, and that is what keeps him going as he sows the seeds of diligence, in hopes of someday reaping the benefits from the hard work, dedication, and preparation.

Professional teams instill much of their habits, routines and aggressive regimens in their training camps long before the season starts. They understand that the only way for a player to excel is to endure the investment of preparation.

There is a story of a professional football player, Walter Payton. He became one of the most prolific players of his generations, and probably of all athletes to have played the game. Payton's success did not start when he wore his favorite Number 34 jersey for the Chicago Bears. His success didn't start, when he broke all records and earned all the accolades. Payton became who he was spending many of his days in training camp, running up and down a hill. It was a task that probably no one required of him, but he had the mind of a winner, and knew what it took to succeed. He knew the value of training.

In the town of Arlington Heights, Illinois, the hill came to be known as Payton's Hill, named after the player who dedicated himself to do whatever it took to excel.

Payton knew that on Sundays, when the crowd showed up to see the game, he would need to run fastest and hardest through other athletes who had also trained in anticipation. Payton's success was not an accident. His preparation, running every morning up and down a hill that probably stretched his endurance beyond what he imagined, is what made him.

Preparation is key. It is said that no one can ever be over-prepared. The same principle is true for when law enforcement personnel are forced to deal with threatening situations that require them to be at their best. There are levels of readiness that they must be prepared themselves for. They understand when a threat is not just another routine 911 house call. They approach danger from a mindset of war, counting on everything they had learned up until that moment. They are united as a team, armed in full gear, ready to defend and attack, if necessary. Yet they cannot do all this, if they haven't spent days and weeks and months practicing their response. They equip themselves for battle with helmets, face guards, gas masks, chinstraps, shoulder pads, bullet proof vests, arm guards, shields, tactical duty belts, kneepads, shin guards, steel toed boots, clubs, and assault rifles. They are prepared.

The training refines their response and their attitude. Regardless of the sport or profession, no one shows up at the scene of the event without their gear. The training transforms their instincts, and they get onto the stage dressed to perform.

The law enforcement personnel wear their gear to protect themselves from potential threat. If policemen are armored to fight men, how much more equipped should you and I be when sparring against Satan, the enemy waging war against our souls (1 Peter 2:11). We can never be over-prepared for a war that is too expensive to lose. This truth should be our encouragement — not our fear — as we fight for our peace, family, kids, friends, finances, health, mind and soul.

All of us understand that preparation is crucial no matter one's occupation. Our focus should be on doing all we can to equip ourselves before the bright lights and long before the crowd of witnesses takes their seats. In football, I learned how the running backs, wide receivers and all other positions have an instrumental part to play, but it is the quarterback whose position is the most critical.

Of all the positions on the field, he has the one-player role. Although he is part of the team, he is set apart because he is in the driver's seat. Even when a quarterback's position is that of a backup, and he is yet to see the field or play in a game, his work is no less important. He understands that in an instant, it could be him jogging onto the field, at the center of the action. So, at training camp, and throughout the training season, even when a player is designated the third string quarterback, he spends his days and nights preparing for a game. He has to be ready.

The same is true in our day-to-day lives. Our training camps may be wherever God in His wisdom and grace have us. He uses the people and the opportunities we come across to refine us. In the quiet and alone, when there is no one to see our development process, that is where God molds us into who He wants the world to see. He prepares us. He refines our talents and skills. He shapes our story. In our training camp, as in the professional athlete's, there is never a wasted moment.

We have to be prepared for greatness if we want to succeed. God wants us to win. Whether we are starters in the proverbial game, a third string backup player, or even a player who is relegated to the practice squad, we must stay prepared. Truth is, we never know when it will be our time to get onto the field.

Nothing of enduring quality is built overnight. It is better to *practice preparing, than prepare to practice.* The task at hand is to stay ready.

THE GREAT GAME IN THE GARDEN

Satan has schemed against you and me from the beginning (Genesis 3:1). He is our opposition, and his hope is for us to lose. The objective of both teams in a football game is to win, and win at all cost. As an offense, you and I must follow the game plan of our head coach. This is why we prepare, so we can hear our coach's voice when He leads. The mission through the game is to gain yards, move the chain, and win games. None of these would happen if we show up in the spur-of-the-moment, and take the field unsure of our assignment.

We ought to know that there is a deceptive defense that tries to deter you and me. In order for their game plan to work, they also study films of every play. They want to learn the tendencies of the offense — you and me — and try to expose any weaknesses. Unfortunately, the rule applies the same way for both teams. The good news is that the offense also has access to the same game film, which in turn allows the quarterback to study the different schemes of the opponent.

One thing is true: the team that wins is not necessarily the team with the best game plan and even the best player, but it is the team that executes a plan to perfection that wins. Our perfection is through faith in Christ Jesus, and through our training, we are made perfect in Him.

There may be more than one strategy that leads to the win, and whether we win in an untraditional and unorthodox manner, or with a simple strategy, God's abundant grace has everything we need to carry us through to an expected end. But you must have an experienced coach.

To understand the mission of the game in which we are involved, we must understand that it is because of the rebellion of Satan that we are in the midst of an ultimate battle for our souls. There is the enemy that wages war against our thoughts, hearts, and soul every day. There is nothing more important than a decision to "Be alert and of sober mind." The encouragement is to constantly guard our hearts because our enemy "the devil prowls around like a roaring lion looking for someone to devour" (1 Peter 5:8).

The enemy uses whatever and whoever to try and stop you and me. Even worse, he will even try to use us to stop our own selves. The real question for all of us to stop and ponder is who is stopping us? Is it our own selves or our enemy? If we are truly honest with ourselves, we will often come to the realization we occasionally tend to even become our own enemies.

There are many times when we attempt to pass on blame onto our spouses, kids and grandparents. Sometimes our unpreparedness for the game ahead of us becomes an accusation against our fathers and mothers. We hear things like "I wasn't raised the right way", "I come from a broken home," "I'm a single parent" and, "I have no education." This goes on and on.

We should not allow the tactical noise of the evil defense to play in our head repeatedly, and overcome our thoughts. Whatever our shortcomings may be, our preparation through God's unfailing hand will help us overcome. The enemy knows who we are, who created us, and how we are wired. The devil knows who our head coach is, he knows His undefeated record, and consequently what we are capable of, but do you?

Good or bad, the opinion of our opponent means nothing. The only two opinions that matters are what we believe God thinks of us and what we think of ourselves.

In the game of the life we live, there will be noise from every direction: noise from the fans, and from the sidelines. The loud music and sound effects will be in our ears every moment. They will be especially loud to confuse the visiting team. The noise often works in the favor of the home team because it is their music and sound that they are accustomed to. We are called to fulfill God's purpose for our lives here on earth — this is not our home turf. We are in the "world," always playing a game as a visiting team, but with Christ as our anchor, we always have the full advantage. The most distracting noise comes from the defense, and this is one of the greatest strategies that the already-defeated defense uses to stop a high-powered offense such as ours.

The devil knows that he cannot stop you and me, so he attempts to attack using his six defensive schemes. He seeks to Deceive us, Distract us, Delay us, Deny us, Detain us, and Destroy us.

He wants to control the thoughts in our heads in order to capture our hearts and to win our souls. Fortunately, our training and preparation guides our hearts from falling for his schemes. This is the game within the game and this game is played in the *dome* of our minds.

The enemy desperately wants to defeat us before we even hit the field. He is counting on our lack of preparation to guarantee his win. If he wins the mind game, he has already won. He knows there is no competition, and that we are fierce competitors. He saw you and me running up the hill just like Walter Payton to strengthen our spiritual muscles and endurance. He knows the coach on our sideline, and he knows we listen to His voice. So, if we want to get in to the end zone, we have to get out of our comfort zones. The work starts now with a dedication to training.

CHAPTER FOUR

MEET THE DEFENSE

TRAINED AND TESTED

Play Call: 2 Ephesians 6:10-17

"Finally, be strong in the Lord and in his mighty power. Put on the full armor of God, so that you can take your stand against the devil's schemes. For our struggle is not against flesh and blood, but against the rulers, against the authorities, against the powers of this dark world and against the spiritual forces of evil in the heavenly realms. Therefore put on the full armor of God, so that when the day of evil comes, you may be able to stand your ground, and after you have done everything, to stand. Stand firm then, with the belt of truth buckled around your waist, with the breastplate of righteousness in place, ¹⁵ and with your feet fitted with the readiness that comes from the gospel of peace. ¹⁶ In addition to all this, take up the shield of faith, with which you can extinguish all the flaming arrows of the evil one. ¹⁷ Take the helmet of salvation and the sword of the Spirit, which is the word of God."

WHO IS THE DEFENSE?

The Bible is descriptive about the enemy and references many names that describe him at his core.

Abaddon: Revelation 9:1

Accuser: Revelation 12:10

Adversary: 1 Peter 5:8

Angel of the Bottomless Pit: Revelation 9: 11

Antichrist: 1 John 4:3

Beast: Revelation 14:9,10

Belial: 2 Corinthians 6:15

Deceiver: Revelation 12:9

Devil: I John 3:8

Enemy: Matthew 13:39

Father of Lies: John 8:44

Lawless One. 2 Thessalonians 2:8-10

Liar: John 8:44

Lucifer: Isaiah 14:12-14

Man of Sin: 2 Thessalonians 2:3,4

Murderer: John 8:44

Power of Darkness: Colossians 1:13, 14

Roaring Lion. 1 Peter 5:8

Rulers of the Darkness: Ephesians 6:12

Ruler of Demons: Luke 11:15

Ruler of this World: John 12:31,32

Satan: Mark 1:13

Serpent of Old: Revelation 12:9

Son of Perdition: 2 Thessalonians 2:3,4
Tempter: Matthew 4:3
Thief: John 10:10
Wicked One: Ephesians 6:16

The enemy eagerly studies our every move. He pays close attention to our likes and dislikes, and we should not for a moment discredit the craftiness of his opposition. The defense fervently studies you and me 24/7.

There is an enemy of our salvation and of our hope that calculates his actions towards our every step, every move, and on every play. Most often when we speak of the devil, we automatically envision the creature that is portrayed in cartoons or movies; the man illustrated in a red suit with horns, a tail and a pitchfork. I believe that representative image that is beautifully conveyed in a manner we can digest without any apprehension, is sponsored by none other than Satan himself.

We live in a society that needs a tangible reason for anything. We know everything, and have found clever ways to downplay Satan's potent schemes and tactics of persuading people to play down on their own intelligence. For a generation that seeks to know anything and everything, it is amazing how little we care to know about the one person against whom you are spending your whole life fighting. He is the defense against everything God has destined you and me for.

Satan uses our own intellect to work against us. It seems the more knowledge we amass in this world, the more confused we become. He is cunning enough to have us believe that we are smart enough to know when we are being misled. Satan was crafty long before he showed up on this earth, but somehow, we have come to trust in our own ability to detect his ways, as if we can do so in our own might. Satan is subtle and sly. The Bible references his calculating tactics with, "Now the serpent was craftier than any of the wild animals the Lord God had made (Genesis 3:1)."

What we ought to know is that the defense wants to bait you and me into doing his will. He wants you and me to follow his ways and deviate from the ways of God. Lest we forget, Satan understands the game; he was once a major player and knows the awesome nature of our Heavenly head coach. Satan is not oblivious to how sweet and powerful God's words are; in fact, he knows what heaven looks like, just as he knows the benefits and rewards that await you and me. Satan fell from heaven and from grace, and caused the first man and woman, "Adam and Eve" to fall too. The more we strive to make forward progress towards the things of God, the more he tries to bring on the full attack, the blitz.

The term *blitz* in football is when the opposing team disguises all their tactics to send all their players to attack the quarterback, instead of dividing their focus on the other players on a team. The blitz forces the quarterback to make mistakes he otherwise would not have made simply because he would be under enormous pressure, the kind that he could not have anticipated. The enemy uses deception. He would love for us to think that we are winning with outward and worldly success, when inwardly we're not playing or living on the level the coach drafted us for. Even when we are overwhelmed on the inside, Satan would have us focus on the shiny veneer of life, rather than deal with the critical details that could undermine our advancement. We may have some of the nicest and finest things in the world that money can buy, but we will have no peace, joy, or satisfaction if the object of our affection has shifted away from what God has called you and me to do.

There is absolutely nothing wrong with having nice cars, big homes, fine dining, and the best of the best. In fact our heavenly coach wants his players to do well and succeed even more. What our tasks demand, at the center of a crucial game for our souls, is to focus on the bigger picture and on our God whose plan for us is perfect and unblemished.

The corrupted coach pretends to have our best interests in mind, when indeed all he intends to do is to kill and destroy. He wants us to have the appearance of winners, offering us synthetic success. His intention is to steal everything from our hearts. The enemy's idea of winning is a temporary fix, a fleeting victory. His formula for winning is seasonal and creates a brief period of success. He makes chasing artificial accomplishments appear to be the best option, and we only realize it was a bad idea after we've bitten the bait, and are hooked.

I told a story a few years ago about my wife signing up for a 24-month premium cable service. The provider's plan seemed enticing. It included high speed internet, a DVR machine, and all the channels that we thought we would need for a rate of $109 per month. We knew also that of course there would be taxes and surcharges, and were willing to still sign up.

After the first year, we noticed that the bill increased to an average of over $200 each month. That hadn't been anything close to the contract we thought we were signing up for. My wife decided to follow up on the agreement with the cable company. A representative calmly informed her unfortunately the discount was for a promotional rate that was designed to last through only the first 12 months. It wasn't a lifetime deal. After the 12 months, the price was to soar to the regular market rate. What was particularly striking was the fact that the deal was not presented in this manner at the time of signing up.

No one at the cable company thought it was a good sales strategy to show us the whole picture. They did not discuss in depth the fine print and details of the offer. The only thing that mattered to them was the benefit of the promotion. It was short-lived, and ultimately was disappointing to us, but we were bound by a contract, and had no way of walking away without huge repercussions. That was a price we had to pay, for a temporary satisfaction that ultimately cost us much more than we would have had to pay otherwise.

Satan follows the same manner of deception. He has an organized system that baits us into a snare. The devil's strategy is not in plain text. His schemes are very subtle at first and then suddenly, they seem like a slow leak in a tire that we hardly notice until the tire goes flat.

There is a powerful truth that Satan has already been defeated, and the victory for us is already guaranteed. The only prerequisite is to walk in the way that God is calling us to. Our job is simple — following the coach's game plan irrespective of how enticing the defense's counter schemes may appear. The only way we can consistently win against the devil and his already-defeated defense is to continue to rely on our coach's game plan and play calls for our lives. The work of defeating the defense and Satan's defensive schemes happens daily.

In the proverbial football game, Satan paces back and forth with a clipboard of his own, keeping track of his progress. He also has the same *go-to plays* that he continues to use to distract us from our destination. He runs the same plays repeatedly, in fact he leans on his top three strategies: "the lust of the flesh, the lust of the eyes, and the pride of life—comes not from the Father but from the world". (1 John 2:16)

Lust of the eye — he tries to appeal to what you see.
Lust of the flesh — he tries to appeal to what you can feel and touch.
Pride of life — he tries to consume you with you.

Warning! We will not be able to defeat the defense with our own intellectual knowledge, and Satan certainly knows that. Standing on God's word is the only guarantee that we will not fall for the ploys of Satan. This is why he doesn't want us to get our hands on God's playbook, the Bible. Satan is busy playing defense, and determined to win the fight for our lives at all costs. He doesn't want us to study the plays — God's word. He doesn't want us to be in constant communication with your Heavenly head coach through prayer. He wants to keep us from acquiring the wisdom and techniques to detect, deflect, and dismiss his schemes. (Ephesians 5:14-16)

I found out very early in my own life that football is a physical sport and that required the proper gear to play the game. In the same way, life is a full contact sport, with the rough pressures from defense to make you and me want to pack up, fold up and move on from our God-given destiny. But we should never give up. Satan's defense wants nothing more than for us to throw in the towel. He wants us to raise the white flag and surrender. He hopes we throw an interception, or fumble the ball in our distress. He wants us to get penalized, and would spend much of his time reminding us of how incapable, unworthy or inefficient we truly are. Satan's hope is to remind us of every mistake, like an instant replay in a football game, just to have us convince ourselves that we are probably not cut out for the task.

For you and me, there would be nothing Satan would love more than for us to turn to alcohol to cope. He would rather we use drugs to get through the day, or even worse, persuade us to give up on life altogether because we do not see any hope in sight. He is pleased with us doing anything that would not bring God the glory. He has seen God's perfect will for each of our lives and his work is to assure us that there is a better alternative. He hopes a young man or woman will choose prostitution and life of drugs and crime, instead of a becoming a gainfully employed member of society. Satan prefers that we turn to the world's way of accumulating wealth, instead of getting a job or owning our own businesses and working a trade (Hosea 4:6).

FILM ROOM

The film room is where the players gather as a team to review, dissect, and study video clips of previous games. This is where they get to know the opponent in detail. The footage is available to every team and individual player. Watching the film of previous games, i.e., game film, is an opportunity to not only examine our performances and mistakes, but also to learn about our opponent. The film room is the place where the coaches analyze each of their players and speak directly to their teams. This is the moment where the coach shows a player what should or shouldn't have taken place in a particular play. In the film room, we get a unique opportunity to reimagine our steps on the field and take a tour through what we could have done differently. The players make all the necessary adjustments, and are ready to get back onto the field to win.

The film room is a time where players can have deep dialog concerning the plays and strategies executed on the field. They can also share their thoughts and give feedback on what they saw. Not only do teams and players watch films, they study them. In the film room, I would imagine that there are notes taken and key points being highlighted. This is all done for the betterment of the players as individuals and for the team as a unit. In the same way that teams devote time to this process, if we want to be the best, we must consistently watch and review our every move, monitor our actions, assess ourselves, and make corrections.

The value of having the film to reevaluate our steps is to know our opponent's every move, know what we're up against, and know whom we're battling. Indeed, reviewing the film of the game gives us a closer look at the opposition in ways we may not have seen on the field. We may have missed moments that only the video clips of our lives – the game tapes – would allow us to see, like the defense's schemes and signals. By studying film we can really get a sense of the opponent's timing, rhythm, and habits.

Away from all the distractions and the busy moments of life, the film room becomes the opportunity to interact with God unimpeded. It is in a prayer closet that we seek God's face. It is in that quiet place that we can be alone to view our game film with God, our coach. It is like having a one-on-one conversation with the coach as he walks us through every moment, what we have missed and all those for which we have triumphed. He listens to the sound effects of our heart, he sees our every thought. There is nothing more uplifting than to know that God continually corrects and encourages us in love. He shows us how to beat the defense and become a great player in the game of life.

THE STRATEGY OF THE DEFENSE

"The thief comes only to steal and kill and destroy; I have come that they may have life, and have it to the full." (John 10:10).

Satan has a system. Yes, Satan is always organizing. Winning in his ungodly system requires studying, preparation, and following Christ's game plan.

Our confidence is built on the fact that Jesus hit Satan with the ultimate play, *the reverse*. When Satan thought he had won the victory, God raised His son Jesus from the dead just as He had predicted to show how nothing can hold back the will of God. No strategy from Satan can stand against God. He reversed everything and confused the defense. Satan did not see it coming. The great thing we are assured of is that the defense doesn't know what strategy our heavenly coach has called for us to execute. Satan and his defeated defense get confused every time we line up on the field. He sees us in our human nature, but if we are to walk in the will of Almighty God, Satan knows that our next move is bound to be a game changer.

The defense uses many tactics to try and hinder you and me. He even tries to use us against our own selves. This method works best when he can get us to defeat ourselves through our own doubts, fears, stress, worrying, struggles, anger, tiredness, lust, jealousy, hate, envy and pride. He tries to find any opening in our offense. If our own resolve through Christ – our offensive line – leaves any of Satan's agents unblocked, they will come through with full attack, because he is always searching for that opportunity (Genesis 4:7).

He tries to hold us hostage with the silent sins, the things that we think no one sees, or knows. These are Satan's most popular go-to plays that he relies on. The shame becomes a hindrance in our lives, and left unchecked, it becomes the gaps the enemy counts on to penetrate our lives. Satan also uses trigger points to try and cause us to lose. He will replay past experiences in our minds to have us feel and react emotional in situations where we should be the most vigilant. These responses come from our senses, so it is our job to be on guard against trigger points that can get us off our game. This is how Satan tries to counter God's plans and plays.

A good example is that of a person on a diet. It is in his best interest to take every precaution to not put himself in a position to encounter foods he should be avoiding. The same is true for a sexual addiction. We must abstain from watching or looking at things that would make us stumble. If a person is struggling to stop drinking, it would be incredibly unwise to spend any of his time in a place filled with alcohol. "Avoid it, do not travel on it; turn from it and go on your way" (Proverbs 4:15).

Acknowledging and dealing with our weaknesses is crucial to ultimately winning. It is important that our thought processes be properly aligned to overcome the unforeseen attacks — the blitz — of the defense. We must study our playbook – God's word – in order to prevail against the trigger points. We must be wise and follow our coach's game plan, and focus all our energy on executing His play calls at all times. We will successfully defeat the opposing team when we identify and deal with the trigger points in life. We can run in confidence onto the field, and play every day with our very best like it's our last.

The defense is very deceitful, and appears in many forms. Satan specializes in baiting and luring us into the ultimate trap, but his divisive schemes never initially look like a trap until we are already lured in. We are the quarterbacks of our own lives, playing the most important position on the field, and Satan's bait is similar to a pass whose outcome we couldn't have anticipated. It may look good in the air, as if destined to reach its target, until it's intercepted.

The devil has a way of convincing us to make that pass attempt – without the consent of our coach – as if it is indeed prudent. It is only when we have stepped away from our coach's intent and taken the bait to throw the ball into the air that we suddenly notice we've been deceived. We can jeopardize our own future and win for a temporary lapse in judgment, and that is all the opportunity Satan was on the prowl for. The defense's goal is to make the play look appealing, and paint a pretty picture when it has been a smoke screen all the while.

There is a way to win. Before snapping the ball and making a decision on a personal play, we should read the defense, in prayer. Staying in close communication with the Holy Spirit — our quarterback coach — allows us to read the scheme of the defense before the play is executed. We can gain yards and reach the goals that our coach, God, has given us. It will only be possible, in His perfect will, by denying the flesh and executing the plays that He has set out for us. Once we pray about the play in private and then carry it out in public, we will gain yards.

We must trust that our heavenly coach has a perfect game plan for our lives, one that is incorruptible and rooted in the ever-living seed of the word of God. Only you and I, if we commit our lives to heeding the voice of our coach, will know what God has spoken to us to work on, and which way to go. Whatever it is in our personal lives that we hope to overcome, God gives us an individual play call to execute. Whatever our challenges and shortcoming may be, we have a coach possessing all we will need to help elevate our game.

Salvation through Christ is the only reason why we get to be on God's team. All of us — it matters not who you are — have once played for the other team. We had been on the opposing side until God's grace found us. We walked in darkness until God's merciful light found us. In our separation from our sinful ways, we are no different from a person walking away from an unhealthy relationship or going through a bitter break-up. We may have left the team, but the memories of our former lives linger still. We would not be favored or liked by our former teammates, who hate the team that we are now on.

The team we have left to be a part of God's team is constantly waging war against our destiny, knowing that God called us into his perfect game plan. Knowing this, it is our responsibility to be alert, not give the opposition anything, have a strong mindset to expose the defense. We do not want to give Satan and his team an inch. Our goal is to shut out the opponent by completely drowning our hears into the will of God.

Job was a great player in this game. If he had been a football player, he would have been nominated as a Hall of Famer. Through his own life, enduring even the most difficult of circumstances, he did all he could to execute God's offense. Even when he was consumed by the pain of his infirmities, he wisely listened to the coach's play calls, feared the Lord and shunned evil. He understood this principle of trusting in the voice of the coach who has formed us in his perfect image and knew us before the very foundations of this earth.

Job was such a skilled player, and even when it was most difficult, he passed every drill that came his way. When he was scouted by the defensive coach, Satan himself, to be tested, Job suited up as a spiritual athlete and forged ahead in faith. It must have been difficult, but he did this one day at a time, and with one prayer after another.

Knowing that the oppressor had been watching game film, stalking and scheming against him, God was still confident that Job would be faithful. God, Job's heavenly head coach, asked, "Have you considered my servant, Job?" God asked this knowing Satan had already been scouting Job. Satan's reply is most reassuring for everyone who determines to walk in the perfect game plan of God. "Have you not put a hedge around him and his household and everything he has?"

The defense knew about Job because they watched his every move. One thing I have learned from many great examples of men and women of faith is that the defense doesn't waste resources on empty targets. Satan and his defense only pursue those who have the ball of dreams, goal, visions and hope. We should not for one minute think that we're off the hook if we're not actively pursuing our dreams and setting goals as God in His own grace is calling us to do. The devil, the corrupt coach of the defense is ultimately against anyone who is alive and breathing.

Our work begins, and now that we know the adversary, the angel of the bottomless pit, the deceiver, the father of lies, the murderer, the ruler of this world, the Serpent of Old, the Tempter, the thief and the wicked one, our work is to hang on fully to the infallible word of God. We know the defense, but he is no match for God – our coach — our team, and the host of angels rooting for you and me.

CHAPTER FIVE

QUARTERBACK

YOU ARE THE QUARTERBACK OF YOUR LIFE

Play Call: Deuteronomy 31:6

"Be strong and courageous. Do not be afraid or terrified because of them, for the LORD your God goes with you; he will never leave you nor forsake you."

For everyone who sits before a television screen to watch a football game, one of the storylines that you cannot help but hear is the nature of the quarterback — the man at the center — the one on whose shoulders the game plan stands. His attitudes and approach to the game set the tone for every other player on the field, and especially how the defense will react. There are often two types of people in the quarterback position: the conservative quarterback and the courageous quarterback

If we had the ball in our hands today, what would make you or me a conservative quarterback? The latter is the kind of quarterback who rarely takes any chances or risks. He is the man who is highly concerned about making mistakes or the play not panning out as he had planned. He is the quarterback who stands on the field not fully trusting in the coach's play call.

Or in that same position, would we have the guts to be the courageous quarterback? Would we be seen as the quarterback willing to trust his instincts, believe what his faith has taught him, take risks knowing that he has all the tools to excel, and follow the coach's game plan to victory?

Can you and I have full confidence in the coach's plays, trusting and allowing him to dictate the strategies that will advance the team? Can we trust that the coach knows everything we do not and cannot know, and has our best interest at heart, so all we have to do is to heed His call?

There is the quarterback whose courage rests on the faith in the one whose voice he hears, even when he cannot see the whole field. He leaves the door open for the coach to have creative freedom and liberty with what he can do with the offense. The courageous quarterback doesn't play in fear and he doesn't play scared — he is fearless. He understands that time is valuable and that every moment must count for something. He is not self-focused. His audacity to win does not come from his own might, but in a knowledge of who he is surrounded by, and he can be confident to pass the ball around to his offensive team every chance he gets. He gets his team involved. This is one of the reasons that courageous quarterbacks have such great success. He understands the underlining principle of being ready, willing, and able at all costs, and at any time to execute whatever play the coach calls in that moment.

In like manner, are you and I courageous enough when it

comes to trusting and having complete faith in God, our coach? Can He call any play he wants in our lives to help us grow and become better? Will we gripe and complain because of our own doubts? Can he stretch us beyond our comfort zones? Can God give you and me a new play to run to broaden our knowledge?

Can we allow Him to expand our imagination as he sees fit, and strengthen our faith to put our confidence in Him alone? Can we trust Him enough to throw the ball where he leads? Or would we rather stand in the familiar, and hang on to any talent and opportunity that God has set ahead of us?

Could we possibly be holding back our own blessings by limiting the number of plays God can call in our lives? Are we the quarterbacks of our own lives slowing down our growth? We can literally be the one stopping and blocking our own success, our own passes, and our own completions. Yes, it could be us!

One thing is for certain: our coach sees the game much differently from us. "For my thoughts are not your thoughts, neither are your ways my ways," declares the Lord. He reminds us that "As the heavens are higher than the earth, so are my ways higher than your ways and my thoughts than your thoughts." (Isaiah 55:8-9)

For everything we could possibly think of, He has seen it all. His perspective is from a different vantage point, one that is not obscured with any fear or doubt. Just as in football, where some of the team's offensive coordinators are always sitting in the sky box high up calling plays, our coaches sit high up, and see every move even before we think it. The view from above allows the coaches and coordinators to see the entire field from a higher perspective. God, our heavenly coach, sees the game from a higher level than us. There is nothing that can be hidden from His sight. For this reason alone, there is nothing more reassuring than to know that we have a coach who sits high and yet sees low, an ever-present coach who sees every possession, sees every play, and every point.

The most powerful and dynamic relationship in the game is always between the quarterback and the head coach. It is his signals that the rest of the team follows, once the quarterback interprets them. The quarterback should trust the coach, knowing that the coach always has the team's best interests in mind. Ultimately, the quarterback who fully trusts in his coach's plays makes himself available to receive all that the coach has for him.

In football, the phrase "buying into the coach's system" is often used to describe a scenario when the player learns to wholeheartedly embrace the coach's plan. Embracing our heavenly coach's system demands our fully submitting to His game plan. Only then will we reach our full potential and be lifted to heights that only God can lead and guide us to. This requires the quarterback to use the most powerful tool that God gives us: faith. We all have faith, but whether or not we actively use it is the key. The Bible teaches a remarkable truth: "Now faith is the substance of things hoped for, the evidence of things not seen" (Hebrews 11:1).

Faith is a complete confidence in someone or something, trusting the unseen facts. Faith allows the coach to dig into his playbook, knowing that his quarterback will confidently execute whatever play he draws up. Faith enables the coach to have a free range of unlimited possibilities.

On the field, there will always be a host of voices coming

from all directions. A quarterback seeking to succeed in this environment must be vocal, loud, and confident. To lead our team, we must be able to effectively communicate the coach's play call in a manner that is as clear to our teammates as it was to us. We must act with precision and hang on to our coach's every word, rather than changing the strategy to align with what we feel in that moment.

Confidence plays a major role in the delivery of the message. The quarterback who has taken the time to study the terminology understands all the nuances. He believes and knows he has the ability to do great things and consistently transcends to the level of assurance that enables him to deliver and execute the play call. He does not trust in his own might, but rather leans wholly in the coach's direction.

You and I are the quarterbacks of our own lives. The great news is that we have a heavenly father, a coach who never slumbers on the sidelines, never loses a game and knows all our shortcomings and tendencies. His system is perfect, and He has each of us in the palm of His hand. He understands our weaknesses, yet He drafted us for this purpose knowing that we are well able to win, in His system.

We must trust our coach. We must come to the realization that He only calls the plays that will put us in the best position to succeed. We know that He has the ultimate outcome in mind, and loves you and me so much that He cares about every strand of hair on our heads. It is on us to believe that He is setting us up for victory with every play call, even the ones we do not understand. He wants to see us triumph, and for anyone who is willing to submit to him, He assures us that He will bring us to an expected end.

In my own life, I am continually learning that we should not be concerned with what play the coach calls for us; this is something we should never ponder. Our advantage is that we have a loving coach who is willing to sacrifice what is most dear to Him for our victory, and that is enough reason to lean on Him even when we cannot explain His plan. One way or another, coaches have a way of getting the best out of their players. It is fascinating how the coach believes and sometimes even has more confidence in his players, when the players themselves struggle to have that same level of confidence.

The coach knows what you and I are capable of. He knows our strengths and the areas of our game that need improvement. The coach sees his players for who they are, and not only as athletes. He also sees our character and willingness to grow and adapt. He sees the greatness and potential in His players, and for every journey He sets us on, He factors in not only our physical skills but also our mental sharpness. These traits were all reviewed when we were drafted, and He alone knew how He would use them to bring Him the glory.

In the same manner our heavenly Coach knows our every move. He knows more about us than we know about ourselves. He sees more in us than we see in ourselves. He knows our values, our worth, and what we are capable of. He knows what's inside of us because he placed it there, and He has a way of getting it out of us. Yes, our Coach in Christ has hidden deep down in each of us great tactics of promise. It will be on us to be willing to dig into them and allow our coach to harness our deep-seated gifts and talents out of us at any time. He only calls plays that He knows we can execute and that will bring out the best in us. We should not be upset when we don't agree with the play call, just listen, and trust the coach. The plays He selects serve a purpose — to move the ball successfully down the field. The play calls get us "first downs" and keep the chains moving in order to score points and win games.

In the end, to be an effective quarterback with courage to win, one must be a giver. God demands the best from us at every turn; He expects excellence and top-tier quality. So how are we operating? Are we playing our best from the *shotgun, under center, no-huddle,* or a *hurry-up offense?*

Which coach is in our earpieces? Is it the heavenly coach or the corrupted coach? Whose commands are we living our lives by?

God created us in such a way that whatever defense we line up against cannot hold us. There is no problem too big for our coach to handle. There is not a challenge that the heavenly coach did not equip us to conquer.

As the quarterback we will learn that it's not all about us. We do not play this game alone. Rather, we have to take advantage of our explosive offensive weapons. Being able to smile in the face of challenges, not allowing pressure to pin you down, loving others, and giving, are all offensive weapons that we have at our disposal. The way we can be an explosive offensive weapon is to know our playbook — God's incorruptible word.

Football enthusiasts tend to say that the best offense is a good defense, but I have come to believe that the best defense is a good offense. Having a high-powered offense that plays at a high level and score points could be just as much of a threat as a highly charged "shutdown" defense.

THE HEAD GAME: IT'S IN THE MIND

The fact is that there are two teams playing in our head at every minute. There are two coaches in a head-to-head match-up. There are many players, but only one opponent. There is a loud crowd with many fans who came to see one team emerge the winner.

We should never allow the enemy to take hold of our thoughts. It is incredibly important to always be accessible to correction from the coach, not shut down correction and embrace change.

As the quarterback of our lives, future, and destiny, we are responsible for our team and its success. We are to gear up with purpose and be intentional about gaining yards, moving the chains, scoring points, making touchdowns, and winning games.

Like the confident and courageous quarterback whose foundation rests in his coach's vantage point, we ought to have poise in the pocket. Like the player who will be expected to go through the necessary progressions and release the ball, our job will be to pursue our dreams, purpose and passion with fearless accuracy. We should not be hesitant to do what God is asking us to do. Instead, we should have a mindset to respond quickly to the promptings of the Holy Spirit — have a quick release of the ball of our dreams and hopes and hit the open man.

If we are to excel down the field, we have to be determined to take a shot and try. We have practiced and trained for this moment, so we have to believe, and execute the play. Even better, we have a coach who guarantees us the victory on our side.

It is the quarterback's duty to delegate and spread the ball through the offense making sure he delivers it in the right place. So it is our work to ensure that the offense thrives and systematically progresses down the field putting the ball in the playmaker's hands. He must be in constant communication with his team about what he sees and hears. Most of this insight is received through the transmitter in his helmet, which comes from the voice of the quarterback coach. The quarterback shares the play call with the team from the coach, shares the ball and contributes in winning games.

As children of the most High God, this is how we ought to operate on the field of life. We will stand on the field ready to receive the play call from our heavenly Father, through his Holy Spirit, and relay the plays to our brothers and sisters on the team. We have to spread the ball of faith and win as many souls as we can.

One key thing is that our responsibility as the quarterback of our lives is that we have the ability to change the game. Our job is to share the ball, which represents the dream attainable through the fruit of the spirit — love, joy, peace, longsuffering, kindness, goodness, faithfulness, gentleness and self-control.

The successful quarterbacks in the football game know that their rating of effectiveness will be based on how many passes they complete. Yes, statistics are always being reported and recorded. They will reflect how many yards, attempts, completions, incomplete passes, and touchdowns you and I are responsible for. The statistics will be the evidence of how many teammates we have helped score points, and get touchdowns. It will be the clear picture of many people we have placed in position to succeed. This is what we play for, so we have to be bold enough to get out there and be the courageous quarterbacks we are called to be.

For every step we cannot see, we are equipped with an all-knowing father who knows everything. We should not be afraid to take a shot down the field, because the opportunity to reach our dreams is still wide open. The greatest quarterbacks unselfishly spread the ball of dreams and aspirations around. What we cannot afford to do is to over-analyze the coach's play call. We might overthink it and talk ourselves out of it, when there is precious second ticking off the clock.

Can we trust Almighty God enough to do just what He called you and me to do? The play may only be there for a moment, so we have to take action when it's called, move when He tells us, and release the ball upon His instruction. We have to play loose, almost unconcerned about the chance of missing our targets. We cannot be stiff, dread making mistakes, and be worried about how every single thing will pan out. With the courage that comes from the hand of God Almighty, we can afford to leave it all on the field.

"But the one who does not know and does things deserving punishment will be beaten with few blows. From everyone who has been given much, much will be demanded; and from the one who has been entrusted with much, much more will be asked." Luke 12:48

The quarterback in a football game is expected to be intelligent and have a high IQ. A lot is expected of him, and he oftentimes needs to react to complex formations in a matter of seconds. The quarterback is given the keys to the team's success and with that ownership he has a responsibility to the entire organization to lead the way to glory.

Quarterbacks not only can throw the ball for hundreds of yards and make fancy passes, but what is most impressive is their ability to multitask, reading the defense and commanding the offense, while listening to the coaches. They also have to tune out the noise from the loud crowds, manage the time constraints, avoid being hit, and deliver precise passes.

We too, just like the quarterback, are expected to perform in the same manner. Playing at a high level in the real world means managing every endeavor of our lives: dedicating our efforts to excelling in work and in school, patiently nurturing precious children God has given us, being present in our marriages, and responsibly handling our finances. We must be prepared to successfully run and score against any defensive formation the opposition may use to slow us down or try to stop us. The enemy cannot stop us unless we let him.

As the quarterback, we must not only have the sight to survey the field, we must also have a great enough vision to mentally view the play before it is executed, literally seeing in our mind's eye what the coach is saying. It is good to hear it, but it is great to see it. This takes a sound mind and a clear conscience. It takes a hunger and thirst to become better with desire and aspiration to become legendary. We have to hear with our hearts and not with our heads. There are game-changing plays that our heavenly coach has dialed up and showed us in the spiritual realm that will immediately make an impact in our play if we hear with our hearts.

While in pursuit of the glory that comes only under the guiding hands of God, we should not compare ourselves to anyone or anything. We should play our game, but be willing to making adjustments according to the heavenly head coach's play calls. We cannot be afraid to embrace change. For years, I've heard, "That's just the way I am," or "That's just the way I was raised," and that's perfectly fine. Some traditions have incredible value in our present lives and are necessary, but we should not let traditions hinder our progress, slow us down and keep us from the things the heavenly head coach has for us.

We cannot afford to become one-dimensional; rather, we have to be willing to make the right adjustments. Most people want to change and become great, successful, dynamic players, but they aren't willing to risk what they already have.

Trusting our coach means knowing that He will not give us the wrong play calls. We must listen intently and we lean upon God's grace and goodness to be our guiding star. Most quarterbacks in the football game may not be successful because they cannot get themselves to trust their coaches. They are unwilling to stop, look, and listen and be teachable by a proven instructor. They would rather run the risk of running their own plays, thinking that from their own experience and skills, they can navigate their way to the next level.

It is very crucial that we remember that there is a higher game plan and system that supersede our personal plays. We should not be thrown off because we don't believe the play call is designed to meet the goal. God in His infinite wisdom might have drawn it up unconventionally, but we can trust every play that God has designed, fits the need of the ultimate goal—to win.

CHAPTER SIX

GAME PLAN
GPS - God's Plans Succeeds

Play Call: Proverbs 3:5-6

"Trust in the Lord with all your heart, and lean not on your own understanding; in all your ways acknowledge Him, and He shall direct your paths."

A road map directs us to a destination, just as a game plan carves a path for players to follow to lead us to victory. With the right game plan, and team has a high chance of winning. With a perfect plan, one that has been masterfully and flawless created since the foundations of this earth, the outcome is guaranteed. That is enough to get excited. We are on the winning team. We are justified and predestined to win.

The most powerful truth we cannot afford to discredit is the fact that we must know whose team we are on and who we are playing for. We rush onto the field knowing that we are on the winning side—God's side. Satan does not want this fact to settle into our hearts on any day, hence he spends his time and energy reminding us of who we are not. The opposition of our future understands that as a quarterback of this game, any confidence we can have in our heavenly masterplan would make us able to make hand-offs of encouragement to others, pass the dream to our spouses, families and friends, and everyone around us.

Satan knows we are most dangerous when we stay in our offensive mindset, with our hearts fixed on the love and grace of the God who called us into his family. Therefore, Satan tries all he can to attack early in the morning, even before we can set our minds on a new day. This could be why waking up and getting our day started could feel more like a chore if we are not careful. Our physical bodies will not automatically calibrate; we have to be intentional. A positive response to God snapping us the ball to wake up is crucial. We should wake up and get on our knees in victory formation, on our knees in prayer. The truth is, if we wake up, we have already won. We have to claim it.

In a football game, when the winning team has secured their victory, they "take a knee," signifying that the game has been already been won, even before the final whistle. What difference would it make in our life if we woke up with that same mindset every day, knowing that Christ's sacrifice is sufficient to secure our victory every new day? We have to walk in it, embrace it, and live it out. Above all, if we have received Coach Christ, we've won.

MEET THE COACHES

A football game doesn't begin without a coaching staff in place for almost every position on the field. The assistant coaches work side by side with the players and help them to perfect their craft, sharpen their skills and teach them new techniques. It is necessary to have specialty coaches who consistently assist players on a one-on-one basis. They are active agents who have professional experience playing the positions they now coach. Their experience gives an incredible boost to the players and adds knowledge and value to the team. The players know that even when their straight is insufficient, this experienced coaching staff is there to guide every minute detail of their lives.

Although assistant coaches play an integral in supporting the team, there are three main coaches that oversee all football operations: the head coach, the offensive coordinator, and the quarterback coach. These three coaches act as one unit and make sure everything runs as designed.

God the Father is our *Head Coach* on the field of life. All we have to do is trust His game plan and listen to the play calls that He drew up before the beginning of time. We must understand who our Head Coach is and His flawless record. He is all-seeing, all-knowing and has all power.

The Bible references many names for our heavenly Head Coach, because he encompasses all things, and he holds many positions. In our own journey to winning, we ought to be reminded every day of the attributes of our Coach. Knowing him and revering who He is through His names will help us understand and appreciate His wisdom and power. He is:

Almighty - Revelation 1:8

Alpha - Revelation 1:8

Author and Perfecter of our Faith - Hebrews 12:2

Beginning - Revelation 21:6

Bread of Life - John 6:35, 48

The Christ - Matthew 1:16

Comforter - Jeremiah 8:18

Everlasting Father - Isaiah 9:6

First Fruits - 1 Corinthians 15:23

Gift of God - 2 Corinthians 9:15

God - John 1:1

Good Shepherd - John 10:11

High Priest - Hebrews 3:1

I Am - Exodus 3:14

Jesus - Matthew 1:21

King of Kings - 1 Timothy 6:15; Revelation 19:16

Lamb of God - John 1:29

Light of the World - John 8:12; John 9:5

Lion of the Tribe of Judah - Revelation 5:5

Lord of Lords - 1 Timothy 6:15; Revelation 19:16

Mediator-I Timothy 2:5

Messiah - John 1:41

Mighty God - Isaiah 9:6

Morning Star - Revelation 22:16

Omega - Revelation 1:8

Resurrection-John 11:25

Refuge-Isaiah 25:4

Savior-Luke 1:47

Son of the Most High- Luke 1:32

Truth - John 14:6

Way - John 14:6

Wonderful Counselor - Isaiah 9:6

Word - John 1:1

God the Son is our *Offensive Coordinator*. Just as an offensive coordinator has the great duty of overseeing the flow of the offense and the players under his care, our Offensive Coordinator ensures than no matter what we confront in the game, it will be well with our soul. He creates the offensive scheme and calls the plays that align with the Head Coach, and puts us in the perfect position to see the victory.

Our Offensive Coordinator puts the team in the best position to win. We have an awesome Offensive Coordinator in Jesus Christ, who has made it possible to play in the game of life.

God the Holy Spirit is our *Quarterback Coach*. He is our means of communication with the Father and the Son, and our wonderful counselor. He speaks into our helmet, into our ears, and into our hearts. His love surrounds us and quells our fears at our core. He stays with us on every play, telling us every play to make on the field of life. If we are children of God, born again into His family, we show our affection by hearing his voice in everything we do.

The Holy Spirit in us is connected to God in heaven through Jesus Christ. Like a device picks up its rightful signal connecting to the equipment, the Holy Spirit is vital for communicating the right play call into our hearts.

During the game, players rarely face their head coach. Still, they always hear his words and play calls. Just as in life, we should always hear our Heavenly Father's play call and confirm the instruction of his playbook, the Bible.

We have to ask ourselves who's transmitting into our helmet of salvation. Without surrendering our hearts and will to Almighty God, we could go through the rest of our lives and not even know what signals we have guiding our every move, whether offense or the defense. What signals are we picking up? We should not let the defense get in our head.

MEET THE TEAMMATES

The fruits of the spirit are our teammates: Love, joy, peace, long-suffering, kindliness, goodness, faithfulness, gentleness, and self-control.

Love is our teammate—We must have love for the game and the players in it. Even if they seem unlovable, this is the most power play in the playbook.

Peace is our teammate. It is available in trying times when the defense of life tries to get us down, pull us back and make us give up.

Joy is our teammate. We ought to have joy no matter what is happening in the game. Never let anything steal your joy.

Long-suffering is our teammate. We may think we should have already arrived at what, who, and where we desire to be on the field by now, but don't give up.

Kindness is our teammate. We can be kind and pleasant. This can carry us a long way on the field.

Goodness is our teammate. Not everyone is good with people, but everyone can be good to people.

Faithfulness is our teammate. We must be faithful in every area of our life, especially in the small plays, for this leads to big plays.

Gentleness is our teammate. Although players gear up and put on a lot of equipment for protection, they are still prone to getting hurt. People put on a strong game-face; they are still acceptable to the hits of life.

Self-control is our teammate. Although we have freedom and liberty, we must have self-control. We should not think that we can get away with doing anything on life's field. In the game, we must not only know the opponent we are playing but we must know ourselves.

In a football game, players must learn and work together with their teammates. The same is true for us in the game of life. Our teammates help us advance the ball down the field and score points. This will take practice, and may not be easy, but it will help us win.

MEET THE REFEREES

Angels are the referees. They are assigned to watch, record, and report everything they see and hear. They are everywhere. They don't miss anything. They are there on every possession. They are present on every play and the amazing twist is that they are on our side.

These angelic referees care about our well-being and welfare. They are there for the safety and protection of the players. The angels are in constant communication with the ultimate officiating crew in the booth. In the reviewing booth, the heavenly host sees everything from the sky cam.

MEET THE CHEERLEADERS

In the game, each team has the opportunity to have fans, haters and cheerleaders. Our spouses, families, and friends are our cheerleaders.

Sometimes our biggest cheerleaders can be our biggest critics because they desperately want to see us succeed. These are the people who see what goes on behind the scenes. They know how badly we want it. They know how much we have studied, prepared and trained for that moment. There may be times when our cheerleaders will say things that don't feel or sound good, but that's okay. We must allow this to make our desire to win even stronger.

HOW DO WE WIN?

One of the most striking reminders we have is that fact that "If you declare with your mouth, 'Jesus is Lord,' and believe in your heart that God raised him from the dead, you will be saved." Romans 10:9

Our dreams, goals, vision, talents, gifts, skills, abilities and strength are, collectively, the ball.

There is no winning without God, the Alpha and Omega. He is the beginning and the end, the author and the finisher of our faith. He is the One who Was, who Is, and Is to Come. A confession of this declaration is the first step toward winning.

If we are able to confess with our mouths the Lordship of Jesus Christ, and believed in our hearts that God raised him from the dead, that is our redemption. For it is with our hearts that we believe Christ's saving grace towards us and are justified, and it is with our mouths that we profess our faith also.

If you're like me you might have asked the question, "How can a confession in the Lord Jesus really save me?" and "What do I need to be saved from?"

I'm glad you asked! It comes from an understanding of who Jesus is. The Bible references Jesus as the Son of God multiple times. Most of us know the powerful words from Scripture,

(John 3:16): "For God so loved the world that he gave his one and only Son, that whoever believes in him shall not perish but have eternal life." Some of us even recite the words without stopping for a moment to ponder their amazing meaning.

One thing we cannot deny is that truth that all of us—every one of us—has been born into this dirty game of sin (Romans 3:23). This is the reason for fallible human beings and an imperfect world. A world filled with hate, pain, sorry, anger, and every ungodly trait. It is a world filled with crime, not because criminals break laws, but because of the sinful nature of all of us. This is why God sent his son Jesus Christ, our redeemer.

WHO IS JESUS?

So, who is Jesus (Yeshua) the Christ and where did he come from? He is the Son of the most High God manifested and revealed as the word of God. Jesus is the one who has been from the beginning, He alone is the chosen one sent from God. Jesus is the Messiah, the Lamb who takes away the sins of the world. Jesus is the truth. Jesus is the shadow of God just as we have a shadow. Jesus is a reflection of God illustrated to us as the son of God. He is a replica of the Father.

For us, Jesus is the ultimate game-changer. He entered the game to change it forever, and sits on the right hand side of God the Father. A perfect God drafted an imperfect player, and sent his son to die a painful death on Calvary to stand in the gap for our sins so that we would no longer be slaves to sin. It is through this amazing grace that we are saved. This is the ultimate plan and purpose fulfilled by the ultimate person.

CHAPTER SEVEN

ULTIMATE HOPE

AN AMAZING GRACE

Play Call: Colossians 3:1-2

"Since, then, you have been raised with Christ, set your hearts on things above, where Christ is, seated at the right hand of God. Set your minds on things above, not on earthly things."

The Ultimate Turnover
Adam turned the ball over when he and Eve were deceived by the serpent causing them to disobey God, the Heavenly Head Coach. (Genesis 3:6)

The Ultimate Plan
God's great game plan is to restore man to his rightful state as

ruler in order to reign and win in life here on earth. (Ephesians 2:13-16)

The Ultimate Play
God sent his beloved son, Jesus Christ, born of a pure and uncorrupted virgin into the world to redeem men from sin (Matthew 1:18).

Jesus confused and defeated the defense! In your rational human mind, the enemy can deceive you to question how the name of Jesus can handle any of your problems. You must understand that the same enemy that has many deceived and addicted to alcohol, sexual lusts, drugs, lying, stealing and the deeds of darkness, is the same enemy who knows Jesus and the power and authority that the name of Jesus has.
Yes, the enemy understands salvation. He knows who Christ Jesus is. He knows what he has done and can do, for he once was a player on the team.

The Ultimate Pass
Jesus Christ was crucified and put to death, so that we could gain life through the Holy Spirit. (John 16:7) Through this, Christ has passed all things to us, and we freely have access to through his Holy Spirit.

The Ultimate Purpose
"But now in Christ Jesus you who once were far away have been brought near by the blood of Christ. For he himself is our peace, who has made the two groups one and has destroyed the barrier, the dividing wall of hostility, by setting aside in his flesh the law

with its commands and regulations. His purpose was to create in himself one new humanity out of the two, thus making peace, and in one body to reconcile both of them to God through the cross, by which he put to death their hostility." (Ephesians 2:13-16).

The Ultimate Promise
"Whosoever calls on the name of the Lord will be saved" (Romans 10:13).

The Ultimate Person
"Where our forerunner, Jesus, has entered on our behalf. He has become a high priest forever, in the order of Melchizedek" (Hebrews 6:20).

There is no one on earth who could have redeemed mankind except the one who created him: God himself, in the form of Jesus Christ. That's why Jesus repeatedly stated throughout His ministries, "If you've seen me you've seen the father. I only speak of what I hear from the father. Carried out through the Holy Spirit, which has been present since the beginning."

Our ultimate hope comes from the declaration of the all-consuming power of Christ Jesus. In order to confess something, there must be an acknowledgement of wrongdoing. The playbook tells us that "all have sinned and fallen short of the glory of God." (Romans 3:23)

There must also be someone to confess to, and we must confess with our mouths. We cannot underestimate the power of a confession from the mouth.

Long before legal contracts and written agreements existed,

deals were sealed with a handshake and your word. These arrangements were considered verbally binding with respect, honor and truth among the two parties. A confession is a declaration, a vow, and an oath. To testify is to be a witness. This is why in the court of law, before taking the stand, the process is for a person to place his hand on the Bible to solemnly swear to tell the truth, the whole truth and nothing but the truth.

It is intriguing to find how the United States legal system makes provisions to prevent people from making any self-incriminating statements. Known as the Miranda Rights, it lists your basic rights when being placed under arrest, regardless of your identity or presumed crime. A person has a "right to remain silent." That was born out of the constitution's Fifth Amendment, and that warning led to the term we know today as "pleading the fifth." The legal system knew this all too well, that the same way our words can get us in trouble or bind us, the words out of your mouth can free you of trouble.

Our mouths and the words that come out of them "have the power of life and death" (Proverbs 18:21). Confessions are powerful because they are a declaration done in complete surrender to the will of almighty God.

Equally fascinating is the word "believe." It is accepting something as true and having an unquestionable opinion on a matter. It is a standalone word, meaning it doesn't need to be accompanied by a supporting cast of adjectives and nouns to convey any meaning. To believe is simply belief, and whether or not we admit it, everyone believes. Yes, every person that has breath believes something.

There are two kinds of believers: there are those who believe that they believe, and those who believe that they don't believe. It's sort of hard to believe, right? Well, believe it! So here we have believers and non-believers. Essentially, there are those who believe in the truth and those who do not believe they believe in the truth, which bring us to the two terms known as believers and non-believers. Nonbelievers unsubscribe to believing, stating that they understand that believing exists, but it's not suitable to them at the moment.

The right to be a non-believer is exercising the freedom of choice, but what happens is the enemy sows seeds of doubt, fear, and unbelief into our thoughts. The seeds are planted so deeply that they seep into a non-believer's heart. It is the same process for receiving salvation, only with an opposite impact. Once we are saved, we are freed from bondage and darkness. This doesn't mean we automatically become perfect, but it does mean we are washed clean and aware. Another one of the devil's strategies is to keep you and me in the dark, because walking in the light introduces us to the truth. "Then you will know the truth, and the truth will set you free" (John 8:32).

FIELD MENTALITY

Rising above and winning require a reorientation of our outlook. We cannot expect a victory if we're playing at a low level. There is a turning point in each one of our lines when we have to do all we can to avoid the mental blocks of the mind. Left unchecked, they can easily become like a mental mine field that causes us to become limited and stagnant. "Let this mind be in you, which was also in Christ Jesus" (Philippians 2:5). Have you ever heard a football commentator make the statement that an athlete is playing at a high level? He's not just speaking of the player's physicality, but also of his mentality, mindset, and mental ability to make proper decisions. In the same manner, we are to live at a high level. It's what separates being good from being great. Every little thing should not be able to touch us. When we live and play at a high level it doesn't matter what is said or done because we have upped our game. We are no longer fazed or concerned with the opinion of the opponent nor do we fall prey to the tactic that's used to try and tackle us. These are all the benefits of elevating our game.

There are many good teams that have skilled players and great coaches, but the mental development of their game still resides at a lower level. They have all the physical skills in the world, but mentally may not be on the same page. But to rise up and win the big game, we would have to challenge ourselves to get through the mental minefields that try to ensnare us during preparation and execution. Without that, we would allow life to slowly slip away from us. We must get into our playbook early, know the tremendous advantage we have, and choose to serve the Lord in our youth.

There may come a time when our circumstances may not make it too easy to do the things we can so easily do now. My prayer is that we don't come to the end of our youthful days and find that we have wasted all the precious time running in directions that have no bearing on our destiny.

A verse in Ecclesiastes 12 frames this perfectly. "Remember now your Creator in the days of your youth before the difficult days come, and the years draw near when you say, 'I have no pleasure in them.'"

We must be mentally tough to win in this league we have been called into. It is a day-to-day battle. In order to win you have to snap the ball from wherever you stand and determine to run the course with full strength. Every snap won't be easy, and every win won't be pretty, but our pursuit of God's perfect will for our lives is too important to be concerned with a beautiful turn. What is important is a meaningful turn. There will be some pushing and shoving, some moving and shaking, some bending and bowing, but there should never be any breaking.

If we want to win, we should be prepared to get scuffed up and bruised. There will be nicks and scratches that will come with our quest for what God has in store for us. It is all a part of the game. We can be confident that the Holy Spirit will stand alongside us the whole time to make sure we are that kind of player and teammate who is equipped for battle. We were not drafted into a team that is feeble. We have not been drafted into a losing team. Our heavenly father stands with outstretched arms as our hope. He is our *ultimate hope*, and through Him we will fulfil our destiny.

This is the reason we were drafted. This is what we play for. It is why we play to win, and winning requires work. Sometimes winning can hurt, but we must be in it for the long haul knowing that we are wrapped in the hand of an Almighty God who will surely bring us to an expected end. We must listen to our Head Coach and the coaching staff, (God the Father, Son, and the Holy Spirit). They know everything about us, and are responsible for placing us in this great game called life. Therefore, it is crucial to have a clear head to block out distractions, and rid ourselves of deceptions and doubts. This will allow us to hear our coaches' flawless game plan being executed through us.

We must trust the coach's play call and know that He alone has every player's best interest in mind. God is not guessing.

Every play has a purpose. He isn't just calling the play in hopes that it works out. He is never on His throne in Heaven wondering why life took unexpected turns. He is deliberate and selective of the plays that he gives us to execute.

It is our duty to stay in our playbook. We must study every detail to stay ahead of our opponent, the devil. Then we go out and execute continuously.

CONTROL THE LINE OF SCRIMMAGE

"Above all else, guard your heart, for everything you do flows from it. Keep your mouth free of perversity; keep corrupt talk far from your lips. Let your eyes look straight ahead; fix your gaze directly before you. Give careful thought to the paths for your feet and be steadfast in all your ways. Do not turn to the right or the left; keep your foot from evil" (Proverbs 4:23-27).

Guarding our hearts and minds often tends to be one of the more difficult exercises we can be engaged in. Maybe the world outside has unsuspecting ways to creep into our lives, and before we know it, we are fighting a battle we could have avoided, if only we were watchful of what we allowed into our space.

Our focus should be on not letting anything that is not designed to move us toward the calling on our lives cross the line. In life there may be things that come across the figurative line of scrimmage in our minds, but we have to be vigilant, and do all we can to keep our face fixed on the coach's voice in our helmets, that instructs the path we should be following. This viewpoint is incredibly important in life, just as in football, where there is always an offensive line whose sole objective is to keep the defense from getting to the quarterback.

The line of scrimmage is where the offensive line comes

face-to-face with the defensive line and the side who typically wins the play is the group that dominates the line of scrimmage. Every quarterback desires to have the best offensive line because it represents protection. It allows the quarterback to have more time to throw the ball and to make the right decision against a defense that's confronting him rapidly.

As the quarterback on God's team we must win at the line of scrimmage, counting on our offensive line to build a hedge of protection for us. The rest of the work will be ours to make sure that we act swiftly in God's will and direction, and not lie dormant and let anything get to us. We are the heart of our team so it is important to be protected. It is also crucial that we secure and guard our hearts from things we hear and see that aren't steering us in the perfect direction for our lives. Our eyes and ears are an entrance that leads to a walkway to the heart, a pathway towards our soul.

Our soul is a gateway that will connect us through eternity with either God or Satan. There is nothing more important than our soul (Mark 8:36). Therefore, it is important to be mindful and be careful about what and who you listen to. You ought to guard your ears and watch the company you keep, because it can influence and eventually shape your thinking as well as the actions you take in life. We must not be deceived: "Bad company corrupts good character" (1 Corinthians 15:33). That is a truth that we have to ponder, remember daily and allow to reside in our soul.

The defense tries many things to get to the quarterback: disturbing his rhythm, disrupting his timing, and slowing down his momentum. He can blitz you; bring an edge rusher or a high safety.

These schemes are designed to confuse and attack the quarterback; the defense want to ruffle and rattle him, but one move that's considered illegal is roughing the passer. This action warrants a flag on the play and a penalty is assessed. Being a part of God's team and of his kingdom, we must know our rights and the rules of the game. Know that the enemy cannot do anything that he wants to us, within the pocket, but if we don't know the rules, he can and he will. Stay within God's game plan. Study the playbook, execute the coach's play call, and fear not because God has us covered.

No one wants to lose. It's the reason some fans obsess, grip, cheer, shout, and become emotionally involved over the success and well-being of their team! They become vested and attached because they feel if their team is losing they are losing, and that is not acceptable. They want their team to have the best players and coaching staff that one could possibly dream up.

They want a team that possesses top speed, endurance, strength power, stamina and chemistry with a winning attitude and spirit. We can relate to the game of football because it's easy to correlate it with the daily battles that occur in our lives and that we must endure to win. There are some great catches and runs, as well as fumbles and interceptions. There are also cries and laughter, but our ultimate focus and mission is to continue overcoming and prevailing to advance and to win like the champions we are.

We must have the resilience and mentality of a player that says, "I can play at a high level anytime, any day, anywhere, and win on the road in a hostile environment, ignoring crowd noise in front of a sold-out stadium." Understand that every fan in the stadium is not cheering for the same team or for our success. We were created to win. We are more than conquerors in Christ Jesus. No weapon formed against us will proposer. If God is for us, who can be against us? No one.

COIN TOSS

Right before kick-off in every football game, there is a coin toss. The coin toss determines which team receives the ball first. As minor a detail as this may seem, this is a probably one of the most important parts of the game. Much so that teams have factored this into their strategy and game plan to put them in the best position to score and win. Everything matters when it comes to winning. As they say in the military, "strap up your boots." An unlaced shoe may seem secondary, but it could mean the difference between life and death. Similarly, in this game, we don't need anything tripping us up or slowing us down.

Think about it this way. A quarterback hits the open receiver, the receiver breaks free and gets down to his goal line but trips on his own shoelace, the clock runs down and the game ends. What in one instant seemed like a small thing could cost the team a chance to win the game and potentially go on to win a championship. By itself, it may be inconsequential, but woven into the big picture, that could make all the difference. We cannot afford to let the small things stop us from getting our rings and trophies in life.

To win, however, we must be alert, watch carefully, and pay attention to little details of our life. The phrase, "The devil is in the details" is a common saying, and simply cautions you and me to pay attention and look for what is hidden upon first sight.

In my professional career, I worked with clever marketing professionals, advertising geniuses, and promotional gurus. They all shared one thing in common. There was always a flow and logic in their thought. There were plenty of seemingly insignificant details that when these experts were selling something, could be both catchy and appealing. However they created their sales pitches in such a way that customers were not overtly aware of the details. The product's benefits were put on display, but unless you paid attention to the fine print, there was no telling what you would notice. For most people who struggle in one area or the other in their lives, it is the details that trip us up. Therefore, as we find in scripture, ". . . in order that Satan might not outwit us. For we are not unaware of his schemes" (2 Corinthians 2:11). Winning takes work, determination, and stamina, but ultimately, it takes the relentless guiding hand of our Head Coach, God.

Winners don't beat themselves up. They show up, run their routes and win with theirs words and their walk, which comes from studying their playbooks. They play boldly and aggressively. They don't panic. They celebrate every great play but are prepared to take on the next. They handle the pressure and tune out the crowd noise. Most importantly, they respect their teammates, the offensive coaching staff, and their heavenly Head Coach. Whether it's blocking, screening or running a route, it matters not, as long as you are in the game and on the field.

The object is for us to be in the Coach's game plan, and for His presence to override everything we wish for, and let His will alone rule.

Chapter Eight

KICKOFF

Enjoy the Game

Play Call: Genesis 2:7

"Then the LORD God formed a man from the dust of the ground and breathed into his nostrils the breath of life, and the man became a living being."

When the whistle is blown to start the game, we should give it our very best effort, from kickoff until the last play. We cannot afford to wait to make a statement in life. Life happens in the very moments that we breathe and our heavenly father has created and called us for this precise time in history. When the whistle blows, that would not be the time when we imagine what being the game would be like; rather that is when the game is actually began.

When God, our Heavenly Coach, starts the game by waking us up, we must hit the ground running. We must learn to appreciate every opportunity that each day brings. We cannot take our waking up to see a new day for granted because not everyone in the world receives that same opportunity. Our presence on this earth for another day is evidence that whatever purpose God has for us, He has another lifeline for another day to bring it to fruition. It is up to you and me to take advantage of the kick-off of a brand new day. Whatever our shortcoming may have been, we ought to appreciate the blessing of living and breathing. Not only must our feet hit the ground, but we must run fast and hard with the football of hope and our God-given talents that He prepared for us long before we were drafted.

God knew our weaknesses before we came aboard his team, yet he called you and me worthy. Now that we are properly equipped and suited up as a spiritual athlete and we know the mission, understand the game and why it is being played, let us hit the field.

As children of God, we are always on the offensive side of the ball. Daily, we are to embrace the privilege of having been chosen to implement the plays God has designed for our lives. Our goal is to make progress, and our mission is to win.

In the same way, as children of God, we don't have to worry as much about a defense or defending ourselves because with Christ we have an unbeatable offense and we are unbeatable. How can we lose a game with a high-powered offense that continuously scores points every time we suit up and hit the field for Christ? Through Christ we can possess the ball, over and over.

Our coach gives us an opportunity to score in every area

of our life that we are willing to trust into His hands. We score points and get wins when we obey the voice of God. From the first kickoff, Adam fumbled the ball, but Christ recovered it and returned it to us. This was the ultimate play.

Just as a quarterback of any team understands the responsibility and authority of his position; we cannot understate the truth and power authorized by the Head Coach. Our teammates depend on you and me to orchestrate the offense, spread the ball, and put everyone in the best position to win. The voice of our Coach is louder in our helmets when we are patient enough to listen and have a genuine heart that is bent on drawing closer to Him.

As children of God, we must understand who we are and the authority and position we hold in Christ. This power comes only from our head coach, God the Father, so we do not have any excuse to not line up and play the game we were called to play.

WINNING ON THE ROAD

If we were to do a survey asking teams whether they prefer to play from home or at home, I believe the answer would be unanimously, for playing at home. There are many reasons why people who play sports want to play in our own backyard. It comes with having the luxury of avoiding the hassle of traveling to unfamiliar places, and having more time to prepare for the game ahead. These are just a few reasons most athletes prefer to play on their own turf. This is the *home field advantage.*

Home games are good and benefit from the familiarity. They are seen as an advantage because the home team gets the chance to operate from their comfort zone, and fans cheer them on. It is in stark contrast to winning away from home. The winning team without the home field advantage doesn't have the same warm reception, and finds itself in a hostile environment. In the game of football, only a few of the most celebrated teams have proven records of winning on the road. Only the best teams can repeatedly walk into a hostile environment, tune out the noise and execute their game plans to perfection. This task is not as easy, but it is necessary.

As believers, we are the visiting team and earth's stadium is not our final home. The days may be hostile, the attitudes and perspectives are unfamiliar to us, yet we are able to win on the road. The all-powerful hand of almighty God keeps us afloat when all else is sinking around us. We become the ship that sails on the ocean, yet cannot sink because we do not allow the water — not even a drop — to find its way onto our deck. We must be confident and comfortable enough to win in dark, hostile, and tough environments. It requires prayer, extreme focus, mental toughness and teamwork.

Some of the toughest teams can go to different stadiums and beat the opposing team, and even win the hearts and respect of some of that team's fans. They win in spite of the opposition. All the conditions may not be perfect and even when everyone is the crowd cheers against them, the focus is fixed on the goal ahead. There are some things that the visiting team must continuously do to be great.

You and I are the visiting team, but with Christ's powerful hand guiding our every step, the evil cannot stifle our progress. Our focus ought to be fixed on the prize, on the cross. Calvary is where Jesus Christ assured you and me that irrespective on the opposition that comes against us, "It is finished." The blood of Jesus paid for our sins in full and that gives us the confidence we need at kick-off.

Knowing how to overcome these obstacles gives us an advantage. For us, having a home field advantage isn't necessarily playing on home turf. Rather, it is when we are able to ignore the crowd noise, stay poised, keep our composure, love others and play together as a team, that we get a home field advantage.

As children of God we possess the ball; this is why the enemy is after us. We have the greatest coaching staff in the world with God the Father as our owner and Head Coach; the best offensive coordinator in Christ Jesus, the most wonderful counselor, and our quarterback coach, the Holy Spirit, who communicates every play in our ear.

Our mission as the quarterback of the team is to march down the field with a fervent passion to fulfil every good and perfect will that God has in store for us.

PRE-GAME WARM-UPS: THERE ARE NONE

In life, there are no pre-game warm-ups. There are no inconsequential moments when we can try our hands at how we hope to live, before we go ahead to do so. There are some fundamental ideas that will help us relentlessly pursue God's perfect game plan for our lives and gain yards on the field of life.

Offensive Weapons
- Pray, eat healthy, get enough rest
- Take time and reflect
- Laugh, live
- Be kind to your spouse
- Do your part

- Count your blessings
- Seek to learn; be a good steward
- Trust yourself, have others' interest at heart
- If there is a need, meet it
- Talk less, listen more
- Care about people
- Find your focus and live in it
- Check your motives
- Always give 100 percent; always operate out of love
- Get excited about other people's dreams

Have some NOs
- No malicious intents
- No jealousy, no envy
- No deceit
- No confusion

Have some Don'ts
- Don't be so critical
- Don't argue about Christ
- Don't have an "It's Monday" mindset
- Don't be ashamed of who you are
- Don't be vindictive
- Don't lead with your money
- Don't throw money at every situation
- Don't carry around a condescending attitude
- Don't be complacent, don't be lazy
- Don't waste your time
- Don't be cocky or conceited

The Be's
- Be urgent
- Be teachable, Be keen, sharp, and vivid
- Be enthusiastic, be committed
- Be excited, Be Responsible
- Be humble, Be a servant
- Be honest, Be unmovable, Be unbreakable
- Be content but not complacent
- Be willing to help
- Be about God's business

The Haves
- Have no fear, Have faith
- Have focus
- Have a cutting edge mentality
- Have patience, Have purpose
- Have a solid work ethic
- Have a pure heart

And remember, a shortcut is a quick exit to the longest route.

POCKET PRESENCE

How are you under pressure? Who are you under pressure? Do you perform under pressure or do you panic under pressure? Do you lose your temper or remain calm? Do you make excuses or find solutions? Do you blame others or do you take responsibility? Do you lie or tell the truth? How you respond under pressure says a lot about who you are in such situations. Though this does not ultimately define your character, it does highlight characteristics.

So again, how and who are you under pressure? Do you panic or perform? The objective of the game for both teams is to win. The defense want to stop the offense and the offense wants to prevail against the defense. One of the most strategic formulas of the defense is to get to the quarterback, because in theory, if the defense can stop the quarterback, they can get to the ball and disrupt the game plan of the coach.

Keep in mind, the defense means of attack is by sacking and rattling the quarterback. Remember, roughing the passer is deemed illegal and a penalty will be accessed on the play.

Yes, the defense schemes include creative ways to bombard and blitz the offense, and they will use any deceptive device or tactic necessary. However, one must not be easily rattled or shaken. The play may not always go as planned, or how you thought it would. No matter what takes place on the outside, remain calm on the inside. Don't fret when one door shuts or when one window closes. It's not as bad as it seems. You still have the ball and Coach God is still in control. So, keep the drive alive.

SCRAMBLING

Do you know how to make adjustments? It is quite impressive when a play does not seem to go as drawn but thanks to the quarterback's ability to scramble outside of his comfort zone, he saves the drive and gets a first down. There will be times when standing in the pocket becomes suffocating and stifling to the progress of the team. Knowing how to handle pressure from the opposing team is critical.

Sometimes you will be able to stand in the pocket and wait for a teammate to get open, and other times you will need to do what is necessary to gain yards. Being versatile is a great attribute when being blitzed by the defense because it keeps them confused. In your life are you versatile? Can you stand still, have patience and trust God as required. What about breaking free and moving beyond the familiar to make a play out of no play and a way out of no way? Even when it may seem that the enemy has all your resources tied up, and all your options are cover, don't stay stuck standing in place. Scramble and make a play.

FIRST DOWN-MOVE THE CHAINS

It is gratifying to be in the moment of the game and see progression. Whether it's a small gain or large one, five yards or seventy-five yards, both are indications of effort, perseverance, and a well-executed strategy. As the quarterback of your life you have an obligation to move the ball down the field. Forward progress is directly connected to the chains that mark first downs along the field.

Moving the chains is the goal while in pursuit of a touchdown. In the same way, accomplish and carry out the plan God has entrusted you to do. As my brother, Terrance Clark, expressed through his vision, "Completing the assignment is a good indication that you are on track to turning your dreams into reality."

Forward progress comes out of an attitude that shows our wherewithal to withstand the opposition. Moving the chains one step at a time even when the rushing winds of the opposition's tactics and doubting words are pushing against us, plays an integral role in winning. We must keep our focus on gaining yards, getting first downs, scoring points and winning games.

MAKING PIVOTAL MOVES

To maintain a successful drive, you must make pivotal moves. If what you're doing is not working, sometimes it is necessary to mix it up a bit. Don't stay in the same formation the entire game. If there are certain people, places, or things that cause you to relapse and lose yards, then you must switch up some of your plays. In the game of life it is all about continuously making the proper adjustments. This will set the stage for you to make pivotal moves and advance to your touchdown.

You must be aggressive about your goals. If you're battling with an alcohol addiction and you pass three liquor stores every day, try an alternate route. If you have a gambling addiction, you should avoid the casino. If gazing at a woman too long causes you to think lustful, inappropriate thoughts, ask yourself if it is worth it and immediately review how you could have done better on that play.

Make the most of every opportunity. Life is a full contact sport. One must suit up, put on the pads, hit the field, and go play. Live and play every down like it's the last. Play the first quarter like it's the fourth quarter and you're running out of time. The truth is that every moment is precious and we ought to be ready to move at the whistle, counting on our God's unchanging hand to lead the way.

CHAPTER NINE

HALFTIME

LET'S KEEP MOVING

Play Call: Philippians 3:13

"Brothers and sisters, I do not consider myself yet to have taken hold of it. But one thing I do: Forgetting what is behind and straining toward what is ahead."

Football has many identical traits to life itself. It seems as though, in our journey, we play the first half every minute and even as we go through our day, get the chance to assess what we did well and what didn't work, regroup and get back out there. What is different, however, is that there will be no 30-minute break for us to stop and catch our breath.

No matter what happens in the figurative first quarter—whether it was a day or a moment ago—God's grace is like a mighty storm that stirs within our soul with the energy to regroup. No matter how far we have drifted away from God's path for our lives, it's not over. No matter what happened to you and me in the first and second quarters, there is a grace that is sufficient for us to carry on. There is a second half.

There is more game to be played and there is still time on the clock. We cannot afford to be afraid or ashamed of how we have played and performed in the first half. We are fortunate to have a coach who is always seeking what he can do through us in the moments ahead, instead of dwelling on the missed opportunities we let go. He knew our weaknesses long before we discovered them for ourselves, and His grace is sufficient for you and me.

It is okay that you made some bad throws. He is expecting us to learn, grow and seek to please Him by excelling in the path He has set out for us. His will for us is that we not make the same mistakes over and over again because He is trusting of coordinators to equip us with everything we need to give our best every time we take the field. What He wants you and me to do is to forget about the plays that weren't executed to perfection. The awful decisions we made in the first half are over. There is nothing we can do differently to change them, and He sees them as part of our growth process. God takes our broken pieces and failures and reshapes us, and mold us again like jars of clay in the potter's hand. Our coach is not busy on the sidelines keeping track of how we start. The only thing that really matters to Him is how we perform today, and how we finish—the final score.

I grew up in Wyandotte County in Kansas City, Kansas. My parents' house sat at the intersection of 61st Street and

Leavenworth Road, on a dead-end street. For much of my teenage years, it was as if my life was destined to be on a dead-end as well.

I was growing up in a rough neighborhood that had become characteristic of communities across the United States where the young men and women were taking to undesirable lifestyles. My most impressionable years were being spent in an arena where we could easily drift into bad behavior. A lot of the older men were hustlers, and the young women did everything it took to make money and display a lavish lifestyle. On the surface, it felt as if that was the best way to acquiring everything that a young man desired. Without any meaningful direction, it seemed like they were exceeding all expectations and living the dream.

Through the years, attending school and committing myself to a lifestyle that my parents were hoping I would pursue fell by the wayside. Anything that demanded hard work and enduring a journey that didn't pay immediate dividends seemed less and less appealing. My mother did her part, always telling me to do the right thing, but there was only so much she could do to show me how to carry that task out as a young man. My father was in and out of the prison system. He also tried to do what he could every now and then, and attempted to point me in a better direction than the path he had walked.

I chose to walk in a path that seemed glamorous, but the operative word here is "seemed." I wanted what was advertised as the fulfilling life. The only advice I was interested in heeding came from the people who I imagined could get me the things that I desperately wanted in life, quickly. Unknown to me, every decision was pulling me away from the will of God for my life.

I chartered my own way, and drifted farther and farther away from God's way. I was busy patterning my journey after the "success" I saw in the neighborhood.

I had a cousin who reaffirmed the path I was electing to follow. He seemed to have everything I wanted from fancy cars, flashy clothes, and glitzy jewelry, and at a young age. He had all the girls too, and was the picture of success to me. Decision after decision, I was losing a game where I had been called to not only play, but excel to make a difference in the world I had been born into. My life wasn't meant to be ordinary, but I was bent on making it extraordinary on my own.

I was involved in different unproductive activities from Kansas City where we lived, to nearby St. Louis, Missouri. My life spiraled out of control as I was constantly changing schools—where I was rarely in attendance—to finding friendship with other young men whose focus in life was no different from my own. There was not one thing we spent our days thinking about or doing that was worthy. But even when I was choosing to throw my life away, there was a God who knew who He had called me to become. He was a steady hand in my life even when I was bent on walking through life on my own. The Head Coach knew all I would become and could become when He scouted me. He saw my weakness and tendency to fall to a sinful nature when he drafted me. He didn't want me to die. God did not want me to end up in jail, as eventually happened to my dear cousin and neighborhood role model.

My cousin, Leeottis Yancey died on November 9, 2004, and had the chance to hear about Christ's salvation, and get back onto the field after *halftime*. There were many more young men and women in Wyandotte County and around the country who may never had the chance for God's redeeming power and a second chance.

The great news for you and me is a reminder in Colossians 3:9 that "...you have taken off the old self with its practices and have put on the new self, which is being renewed in knowledge in the image of its creator." I thank God for his amazing grace that saves whatever wretch we have made of our selves. I had to remember that I am surrounded by the arms of an almighty Father who liberates us from the bondage of sin and misdirection, and sets us on a path to fulfil our destiny.

WHERE ARE WE ON LIFE'S FIELD?

In a football game, the first quarter is a time where the players execute everything they've practiced and reviewed. This is their opportunity to make a statement early, to put into action the things that they've learned. As the quarterback of our teams, we are looking to immediately advance and accelerate, moving the ball of hope up the field as smoothly and timely as possible. The idea is to put the team in the best position to gain yards, move the chains, acquire first downs, get touchdowns and win games.

Wherever we may be on life's field, it's never too early to make a play, neither is it too late. It is wiser to make a play in the first quarter, because, the sooner you make a play, the sooner you can enjoy the game. Making a play early allows us to focus on other attributes of the game instead of wondering whether the game clock is working to our disadvantage.

One of the biggest mistakes I made early in my life was to allow material things—all of which have superficial value —to

measure the score. Money should not have been the final authority or standard to determine the scoreboard or the outcome
of the game, but in the absence of knowing my God-given
purpose, anything else had the chance to define my purpose.
The team that makes the most out of their possessions wins.
If our lives are clothed in God's saving grace, we take the field
with the most powerful force on our side. We would be best
served to assess where we are and see if it is working according
to God's perfect will for our lives, and review the game plan for
the second half. Every new moment and new day we have is a
chance to reset and relive. Be encouraged.

Jesus's friend and disciple, Peter, lived a life that many of us can
relate to. He didn't live in his weaknesses, but reminded himself
over and over whose team he was called to be a part of. He walked
on water to demonstrate his faith and denied Jesus when he feared
for his life, but he got over his mistakes. It must have been incredibly difficult but he had to remind himself over and again that the
same Jesus who tuned water into wine was capable of taking our low
moments and using them for his glory. The same man who did the
unthinkable and denied Jesus, was the same person who would go
on to do the miraculous and walk on water.

It's the same way in our lives, that no matter what we have
said or done, there is still hope. There is a pure love that pursues
each one of us, seeking that we turn our hearts to live in God's
will and to please Him. He delivers us from stumbling if only
we can keep our eyes on God. Through Christ's precious blood,
even when feel broken and like we have come to the end of
ourselves, we get a new life from the ashes we have become. We
get another chance to take another snap because we have been
bought at a price.

Age doesn't matter. We are never too young or too old to be used by God as an offensive weapon against Satan's defense. The professional career of a football player may not seem as long as other careers, but there are players who remain in a league for years. They may not be as strong or as fast as they used to be, but they still carry a wealth of knowledge and experience that rookies can learn from. These players are veterans and some are headed toward a Hall of Fame. Likewise, in life, we ought to take heed of those who have already paved the way for us to win in the game of life. They know something we do not, and it is their counsel that can steer us into making some of the most crucial plays in the next moment.

The length of a football field is 100 yards from one end zone to the other. At birth, we all start in our own end zones with the opportunity to run with the ball of dreams, goals, visions and hope. As we age, we learn to move the chains of life and continue down the field in order to score and win.

After the ball is kicked-off some players take a knee, which advances the team's start to the twenty-five-yard line. As we strive to advance on the field, there are plenty of learning lessons. So we have to learn to appreciate every aspect of the game. Each yard gained shows growth and development. While moving along the field of life it is of great value to have a keen ear to hear God, our Coach. We must keep our heads high and our eyes on the ball. Yesterday is gone, and so are any missed opportunities. All we can do now is to dust ourselves off and get back on the field. There is an amazing grace for that.

A PLAY AWAY

I recall watching the play-off game a few years ago between the Baltimore Ravens and the Denver Broncos. Both teams were playing at a very competitive level, in pursuit of a championship title. Denver led the game with a little over three minutes remaining in the game. Baltimore took their turn, with only four seconds left on the play clock.

The defensive players brought all the pressure they could muster to disrupt the quarterback. Just before they could get to him, he stepped back to throw the ball to his player who was running up the field. He had managed to maneuver away from the defenders and it looked like there was no way he would miss the golden opportunity.

The talented receiver, Jacoby Jones stretched out his hands as best as he could to catch the ball. What at first seemed like a guaranteed catch, fell down on the field, much to his disappointment. Anyone amidst the field could see the dejection in his face, wondering how he could have missed an opportunity.

The play ended, Baltimore turning the ball over for the Denver team to have their turn. What looked like the closed curtain on their season ended up becoming a remarkable turning point in the game. The Denver fans screamed and began to celebrate what appeared to an inevitable win. But the Ravens leaned on one central lesson in life, that they were just a single play away from reclaiming their opportunity.

With just about a minute to the end of the game, they got the ball from the opponents. It was the chance they had been looking for, but for a moment it felt as though it might be a little too late. They had to score quickly, against a formidable opponent who was not looking to lose. With 42 seconds remaining, the Ravens snapped the ball and the quarterback scrambled the best he could. He looked down the field and lo and behold, it was the same Jacoby Jones who ordinarily would have given up on himself after the first oversight, who was down the field. He had fought his way amidst the toughest defensive players who were pulling him back with all their might. Jacoby made his first and undeniably outstanding catch of the game. It was a 70-yard touchdown that went on to win the game for the Baltimore Ravens.

Had Jacoby not missed the first opportunity, maybe the team wouldn't have had to dig deep for their own resolve. Had the team not stretched their own faith to believe in what they could accomplish together, maybe Jacoby wouldn't have tapped into the courage within himself to do the unthinkable. For anyone who sat back to watch the entertaining game, the lesson is: it should transcend football.

In much the same way, our pursuit in life's game is strengthened with our team mates – the fruits of the spirit, and made perfect under the guidance of our Head Coach–God. His game plan is perfect, and if we can live in His will to fight through one more play, we can be confident that we are just the next opportunity away from our fulfilling end. We are confident in the truth that the God who began a good work in you and me will be faithful to complete it, but it is on us to trust wholeheartedly on where he is leading.

Never mind the dropped pass. In many of life's challenging moments, it may take some scrambling and fighting all we can to break free. As children of God, we rest assured that there is no challenge that confounds Him, and no limitation so debilitating that we cannot recover. In fact, we may just be one play away from our greatest moment. What we have to do is to shake off the dust from the past and get ready to run out onto the field again.

As players for God, we must know and be open to His direction even when it is vastly different from our own. The danger of trying to run our own plays oftentimes results in our playing into the hands of the enemy.

I think back to my own life as a teenager, sneaking away to smoke marijuana thinking I was the most popular guy in the area. I loved the attention, no matter how short-lived it was. I did not have any use for it, but it was a habit I had picked up because of my environment. We sat back and lavished in the temporary high it seemed to give. I liked it, but I knew in my heart that it was slowing me down from progressing in life. I wasted long days doing nothing, when there were a hundred things God had laid before me to pursue.

I did all the things I had no reason to do, and spent my precious time in places I had no reason to be. The player God had called even when I was in my mother's womb had decided to ignore the calls of a loving coach who wouldn't give up on me. I was acting out of character, the character God had woven me to become. Deep in my heart I wanted to stop smoking, but I couldn't quit. I felt powerless.

There wasn't a day that I didn't hear God's still small voice nudging me to let it go. I would pray in private to turn my life around but in public I would put on a façade to hide the wrestling deep down inside. I had a Coach whose voice was clear in my helmet, but there was a crowd whose noise tried to drown out my Coach's voice. I desperately wanted to quit but didn't know exactly how to go about it, until I became honest with myself before God. God was telling me it was time to get back onto the field, regardless of how far I had run from His plans for my life. The wasted moments were a quarter of a football game that I couldn't get back, but there was another quarter ahead. There was still a life ahead for the redemptive power of God's grace and mercies to get me back on track.

My heavenly coach was always setting up a play call against what the defense was scheming against me. Once I received the play, it was my job to study playbook and understand that I had to confess and come clean with the truth. The truth was I thought I liked smoking, but it wasn't good for me. Doing things that are not good for us can seem to be enjoyable for a short period. It's the same reason people clamor for fast food. It smells good, looks good, and the price is often cheap. The question we ought to be asking ourselves is, "How can something with all these great benefits be offered at a low price, and be beneficial overall?" This is precisely how sin works. It looks good, smells good, and appears to taste good. It's a quick fix that gives the illusion of a fairly low price, but, in reality, it can cost you everything.

I am fortunate to be able to share that you and I can overcome the sinful desires of the world and the flesh, if we allow the master's hand to mold us into who He wants us to be. I confessed and asked the Lord to take the desire away, and that the play I prayed for in private I could run successfully in public. It wasn't easy, but I am incredibly grateful that with God all things are indeed possible. Whatever personal or private plays the Heavenly Coach has drawn up for us, it is our duty to have the conviction to carry them out in public.

If we can be truthful with ourselves, only then can we win the war within. There is a winning spirit and attitude of never giving up like Jacoby Jones inside every one of us. When we think we may have missed what we thought was a great opportunity, God calls us to hang on for one more play. What we may have thought was the end of our story was only the beginning, and the Coach who indeed knows all things knows exactly how to transform our tears into joy to bring Him the glory.

CHAPTER TEN

BEGIN AGAIN
Never Too Far Gone

Play Call: 1 Corinthians 1:27

"But God chose the foolish things of the world to shame the wise;
God chose the weak things of the world to shame the strong."

I remember going to the movies with my mother as a young boy. Nothing fascinated me than when right in the middle of the film, everything faded to a black screen. I anxiously followed every movement, engrossed in every action. As a child, my mind had processed the sequence as one that should have an image on the screen at every moment.

So as a young boy, I was unsure of what to think the moment the screen briefly went dark. A part of me was disappointed to see the movie end so suddenly. Anxiously, I would ask my mother if the movie was indeed over, and she would always smile and say, "It's not over." Those reassuring words are what many of us yearn to hear when it seems we have deviated from the path on which God has called us to walk.

It is never too late for us to begin again. Especially when our hurting hearts seems to have left us in a dark moment and we wonder if the dark screen on our lives means it is over. But as with my mother's comfort, you and I can be rest assured that there is a coach who is so confident of the outcome of our lives that nothing we go through takes away the love He has for us. Like the football player who is desperate for a glimmer of hope, it doesn't matter where we may be on the field; the objective of scoring a touchdown is still within reach.

What if the ball is on our 25-yard line and it seems that we have a long way to go? What if the opposing circumstances have shaken everything within us and we are looking for a hope to carry us, because we feel like we are walking alone? If only we knew that we are not on our own, no matter what we feel, we can find the strength to get started and not compare our field position with others.

What is important is that we are on the field and in the game. Our focus shouldn't be on anything else because we have a Head Coach who is always on the move, even when it seems like there's a dark screen. Our job is to learn to not fret over what we don't have, and rather focus on the skills we possess, and through which God wants to use you and me. There are many times when the very things that we think we are lacking in life become the reason why we are qualified for the position. When it seems like we cannot see the hand of God on our lives, even then, we have to make a choice to begin again.

On our journey to begin again we have to accept and embrace the player God has called us to be. We will not allow stereotypes to rule our thoughts, exclude us, or count us out. God knew our imperfections long before we became aware of them, and He still knows how to use our lack for our benefit.

If we can dust off the dream we tucked away, we can begin again. If we can hang on through another wild day and put our pads back on, we can begin again. If we can navigate through the chaos and woes caused by the enemy and lace up our cleats, we will be ready to begin again. God's plan for our lives may start with the courage to walk back into a school we once dreaded, to change careers to follow something we are passionate about and is more rewarding, or to have the nerve to restore a relationship or family that is broken apart. Go for it.

GO DEEP

The Head Coach who moves mountains is asking us to throw our ball of dreams deep instead of hunkering down to play safe because we cannot imagine what awaits us downfield. Jesus Christ is asking you and me to go deep.

There is a story in Gospel of Luke Chapter 5, where Jesus stands by the Lake of Gennesaret. There the people gathered around him to hear the good news. Two boats sat at the water's edge. The fishermen who owned them were busy washing their nets. Their night's work hadn't yielded much, and they had come to believe that that that is all they could do. Jesus got into one of the boats belonging to Simon, and sat down to teach the people at the shore.

The miracle happened after he had taught, and asked Simon to, "Put out into deep water, and let down the nets for a catch."

Jesus know they had done all the work they could and still came away empty. Simon answered, "Master, we've worked hard all night and haven't caught anything. But because you say so, I will let down the nets."

When they had done so, they caught such a large number of fish that their nets began to break. They signaled their friends at the shore and in the other boats to come and help them. In what seemed like an instant, they filled both boats to a point that they began to sink. That is all it takes; all we need is a willingness to follow the play call of a coach who knows much more than you and I can imagine.

When Simon Peter saw this, he fell at Jesus' knees and said, "Go away from me, Lord; I am a sinful man!" We learn that both he and all his companions were astonished at the catch. Jesus, certainly knowing what was running through the hearts of the men turned to Simon Peter, 'Don't be afraid; from now on you will fish for people.' So, they pulled their boats up on shore, left everything and followed him." That was the turning point that made the fishermen fishers of men. Their lives were no longer the same and never again to be ordinary.

We may have travelled a long way on our individual journeys in life, but could it be that without the hands-on the Almighty God guiding our steps, we have been travelling the wrong way? Jesus told Peter and the disciples to launch back into the deep, after they had spent all night doing what they thought was exactly that. It doesn't matter how deep we think we are or how long we have been doing something; when the Lord speaks, we can go deeper, and we can begin again.

For Peter and the disciples, it was only upon their obedience—even when they count not understand Jesus' request—that they hauled in more fish than their boat could contain. When we listen to God we will be able to see beyond the shallow surfaces of life's events. As a quarterback with a team's success riding on our shoulders, we have to strive to see what the Coach sees. There is a God who is merciful and faithful, and we can be confident that whatever He said He would do in our lives, He will do it. We have the ball in our hands, and he is asking us to launch it into the deep. Can we trust Him to do just that?

You are I ought to remind ourselves that we are game-changers. If we are breathing, we are winning, and we should be encouraged to not be afraid, but instead, to begin again.

I tell the story of a relative who had his fair share of a troubled past. For many of his adolescent years, he had multiple run-ins with the police. It began with minor offences, and gradually evolved into misdemeanors. It was as if there wasn't a week that went by without his clashing with the police or being wanted for one pretty crime or another.

Once he had to appear before a judge in the local courthouse. The charges were read, and with every one of those accusations, it was as if there was a voice that was assuring him that his life would be over. The judge looked down at his checkered criminal record and thought he deserved to be locked away in prison for twenty-five years.

My father presented a letter of appeal to the court, in a last-ditch effort to have the judge give my relative another chance to become an upstanding member of society. Luckily, the judge showed mercy and reduced his sentence to 12 years. After he served his time he was released, a free man. The inmates with whom he had spent several years nicknamed him BO, which stood for Break Out. But after he was released, I renamed him

BA, the acronym for *Begin Again*.

Leaving prison was to be season of new beginnings. It was a fresh start. He had an opportunity to retrace his steps and avoid the same pitfalls that landed him in prison. He knew that the journey would be difficult, yet he was determined to give it a shot. He couldn't—in his own might—see the end goal from where he stood. There were many times, I could imagine, that he felt dejected and thought of giving up. But he didn't.

Winning doesn't always look good. We have all heard of the saying, "Quit while you're ahead." Applying that quote to our lives, why would anyone quit when they are winning? Life demands that we never quit, and urges you and me to rid ourselves of the worldly mindset and stay in the game. If the voices we hear in our helmet come from the God who makes all things beautiful and possible, it is only a matter of time before our ashes, that seem lifeless, get a new lease on life.

As spiritual quarterbacks engaged in the most important game we play in every day, we have the privilege to see the field from a different vantage point. If we accept the call to be born again to God's family through salvation, we have an incredible advantage even in our shortcomings, because we can have confidence in the outcome of the game, in comparison to the other players' viewpoint. Satan and his defense can only scheme, plot and react, but they have no insight into the outcome. We have an upper hand. Our advantage is simply being Christ-like. It is an amazing thought to know that if we are guided by the love and grace of a perfect God, we have the ability to interact with heaven and earth at the same time, all 24 hours in a day. This access is made possible by our Head Coach and Offensive

Coordinator through the gift of the Holy Spirit.

In my own journey, I find it refreshing to rely on a promise Jesus left for you and me, that, "Very truly I tell you, whoever believes in me will do the works I have been doing, and they will do even greater things than these, because I am going to the Father" (John 14:12).

The key ingredient of being a winner is knowing God. Not knowing about Him, but knowing Him. It is a relationship through Jesus Christ His son, rather than a casual familiarity. A winner is someone who does not quit. A winner is made of tough stuff. No matter how many times it looks like something will not pan out, the winners manage to see their way through. They can only stand on their feet again because there is an abundant grace for any and every hurdle.

Winners count on an inner steadfastness and a doggedness refined by the trials of life. No matter how many times the winning quarterbacks are sacked, they manage to get back up. They find a way to play and shine bright despite their conditions. They acknowledge the obstacle but do not spend their energy complaining about the play call. They dare to defy all odds, even when they have to fight ahead in pain. They know that they will win, because they have a faith that rests in the same God who resurrects broken pieces and restores the wounded.

Winners know that no matter how bleak their circumstances may be, they will soon come alive in Jesus Christ, and stand to declare victory. The winning quarterbacks will not take "no" for an answer, because they have surrendered all they are into the hands of an Almighty God who makes beauty out of imperfections. The winner trusts the Coach one hundred percent.

One of the powerful attributes of winning quarterbacks is their dedication to studying their craft. They do not walk away from what got them the advantage because they are ahead. They stick with the coach's game plan. They seek to execute it better every time they take the field. Their desire is to master every detail and in turn be able to embody everything the coach intends to display to the crowd of witnesses. Even when we are winning, that is when we should seek to stay in our playbook, God's word. Our play book is alive and active. It is the dependable word of God.

There are times when we can overthink what it takes to win, and beat ourselves up. The text within the playbook makes it simple; it's about the application and going back to the basics. There is nothing more complicated about doing what we have already been doing in order to continue winning. We have an opponent called the devil. His sole purpose is to destroy us on every down. Knowing this, we cannot afford to casually walk across the field. Instead, we have to be courageous, deliberate and direct when dealing with an aggressive defense.

I recall a time when I played with my little nephew who was pretending he could fly like Batman, a comic book hero. He jumped off the couch and wanted me to catch him. He was so sure I would catch him that he began to jump before I said "go." I thought I would make it a little interesting so I took a few steps back, and without hesitation, he still jumped. I looked into his face. It was full of excitement as he anticipated the next jump.

I stepped even farther back and he said asked, "Are you going to catch me?" I nodded my head yes, and that was good enough for him to take a bigger leap of faith. He was willing to take me at my word, and lean wholeheartedly on what I had told him. In his own strength, not even his pretending to be Batman could help him jump that far, but that wasn't his focus. His focus was all I told him.

I pondered for a moment that even though I had not given him too much of an assurance that I would catch him at a longer distance, he still jumped. My nephew knew one thing—I love him. He knew that I wanted the best for him. Even more intriguing, he had convinced himself that if I caught him one foot away, I would be there to catch him at two feet away. If I caught him at two feet, I would catch him at three. In like fashion we must trust God. He didn't let us fall last time, surely he is not going to allow us to fall this time. The question is, "Are we willing to jump?"

If we want to jump to higher heights we must believe that our Heavenly Head Coach has called and designed a play just for us. He knew our strengths long before he scouted and drafted us, and designed exactly what we needed to excel. We must trust in Him, because we cannot thrive in a system where deep in our hearts, we don't fully believe in the capabilities of our Head Coach. If we cannot wholeheartedly believe that He loves us unconditionally, we in turn cannot wholeheartedly display our love for Him. We will convince ourselves that He is too far away to catch us if we fall.

What is our reason for not making a play for God, our Coach?

If we want to fly like the eagles, we must be willing to spread our wings.

If we want to win the game, we must take the shot.

If we want success, we must be willing to sacrifice.

If we want more, we must be willing to handle less.

If we want to become rich, we must be willing to become poor.

If we want to make it big, we must be willing to start small.

If we want smooth sailing, we must be willing to weather the storm.

If we want it all, we must be willing to risk it all.

Jesus is asking you and me the same question he asked a sick man lying in the corner of a city. Jesus learned that he had been in this condition for a long time —for thirty-eight years, and asked "Do you want to get well?" (John 5:5-6).

The ultimate question you and I must answer is, "Do we really want to win?"

IT'S HOW WE FINISH

In a nationally televised game, the commentators forecasted key players who would have a breakout year at the beginning of the season. It was a Thursday night primetime football game, a divisional matchup between two undefeated teams who were rivals: the Kansas City Chiefs and the Denver Broncos.

As the Chiefs took the field, the commentator predicted that this would be the year they could go win all their games and even play in the highly coveted Super Bowl championship. As the game continued, the Chiefs dominated the Broncos and were living up to their early season promise. The Broncos kept fighting and eventually tied the game with only a few minutes to the end. The Chiefs were in pursuit of a field goal, but fumbled the ball.

Denver recovered the ball, ran into the end zone for a touch-down and won the game. The dejected Chiefs went on to lose the next four games, and halfway through their season, it was as if all the early season predictions were hopeless. For many observers, hope had flown away from the Chiefs. But, unknown to may outside the team's locker room, they never lost faith. They had told themselves a simple story—that the promise of the magnificent season was still beyond reach. Sure, their record wasn't as they hoped, but they had a chance for a new season if only they could imagine the season was starting over from the moment they were in. What if their season was starting again, and all the games they had lost didn't count? The Kansas City Chiefs went on to win the next ten consecutive games. The once unlikely Chiefs team ended up in the playoffs.

Maybe the Chiefs had a coach who was adamant that their season's goal not vanish simply because of the early season's mis-steps. The losses didn't define them. They could leave behind their regrets and trust that a new life could be formed from the ashes if only they trusted their game plan that brought them to the height in the first place. They could begin again, even when it looked like they had blown the opportunity. How we start is im-portant but how we finish is what probably defines you and me.

In life, we come across people who may seem to get a great start in the marathon, while others seem to have started at a slower pace. The key is to never lose faith and hope because no one can afford to lose a game when we have a perfect Coach who assures us that we can start over, and trust Him again. We must dust ourselves off, refocus and stay touchdown bound. We can stand and declare and decree that our second half will be better than our first half.

God is asking you and me to dare to *begin again*.

CHAPTER ELEVEN

PLAY CLOCK

THERE IS NO TIME TO WASTE

Play Call: John 9:4

———————

*"As long as it is day, we must do the works of him who sent
me. Night is coming, when no one can work."*

A football game is made up of four quarters, fifteen minutes
for each. Although there are only fifteen minutes in a quarter, most often the quarter lasts anywhere from more than 20
minutes to even 60 minutes. A lot of unforeseen events happen
within that time span—time outs, penalty flags, two minute
warnings, and referee reviews. It is all part of the game.

For all of these, however, the play clock stops, but what
seems like an inactive moment doesn't mean an idle team. Even

when the play clock seems to have stopped, there are teams and quarterbacks using that moment to get additional information from their sidelines and coach. The clock may have paused, but until it restarts, there are so many things that happen behind the scenes, and you find that the players do not for a moment imagine that the game has stopped.

It is of great delight to know that on a much larger scale, our God, who reigns over every minute and moment, is reviewing every one of them. So, when we look up at the clock and see that there are a few minutes remaining in the first quarter, we must not lose sight of the truth that the other quarters could take longer.

There are two types of time to be considered in the game—the game clock and the play clock. After every play, the clock is reset to twenty seconds, when the player must initiate an activity. In life, we should know there are also two types of time—chronological or sequential time. This is the time the world operates on. The other is Kairos, the time that has no schedule. It is out of this world, the New Testament word which translates to mean "the appointed time in the purpose of God."

It is the time not restricted or limited to zones, days, weeks, months, or years. This time is Divine. This is the time that's acknowledged by God. This is the time He operates on, which is perfect. God our father operates from the headquarters of heaven and holds all time (both chronos and Kairos) in His hand. His time is not our time and His ways are not our ways; so, our focus should be on executing what our Coach is instructing us to do, not watch the play clock.

We must get time on our side. Just as in a football game where the defense approaches like a rushing wind, we do not have all day to execute the play. Time is on our side when we accomplish the goals and dreams that our Coach gave us.

When we start the first quarter off right, we can run out the clock and run the time down by executing the plays of God. We do this by doing everything that is pleasing to God—living the best we know how and making our moments count. It could be anything from spending time with our family and helping in the community, to serving others. We should not hesitate to gain a great lead in the first quarter of life. This is the strategy of a winning team.

Yeshua (Jesus) as a young man had a sense of urgency, and knew very well that what was most important was his Father's business. We can only imagine how he walked the streets of Nazareth as a young boy with pep in his step, fully aware of his mission and what he needed to accomplish. The Jesus who became our living example did not allow anyone and anything to stop him from carrying out God the Father's game plan. He understood the play from the beginning; in fact he was there when it was drawn up, so the urgency of every second wasn't lost on him. He knew that he was called by the Heavenly Father to show up and do his part.

All the way to Calvary to die for your sins and mine, Jesus knew that the play clock was ticking and the game of life was on the line. He knew that time was precious and He had to stay on schedule. He knew what He was playing for. He knew the ultimate plan and that he would make the ultimate play for the ultimate purpose and promise. He knew that he was the ultimate player to save the team and win the game.

So, the question to you is . . . Do you know?

Do you know your mission? Do you know the game plan? Do you recall the play? Do you know your purpose? Do you remember the promise?

Just as Jesus was about the Father's business, we are to be in tune and in coordination with our Head Coach, God the Father. We should be aware of the plan He has in store for each one of our lives, and heed to His play call on every snap. It is extremely important for us to always stay in communication and listen closely to our Coach's calls, because only then can we be sure we are pursuing the dream He has designed for us.

We see how in crunch time, when the game is on the line, it appears that the team's single focus is to get the ball in the best player's hands. If we are a part of God's team, scouted and drafted for a time like this in history, can God count on us to make a difference in the world in which we live? Are you that playmaker? Can God trust you with the game on the line? God trusted Jesus, and He is looking for people like you and me who would be willing to execute an unblemished play call in the same manner. This is the reason we were created (John 14:12).

Keep quiet, but keep working. Football fans understand the saying, "Shhh . . . keep quiet; the offense is at work." There is a time to be loud and a time for silence, but during that period of silence you still need to be in communication with your coach and teammates.

Likewise, time is needed to achieve our goals. The passage of time is subtle, unnoticeable, and wrapped in the mundane. Time is not rude or loud; rather it just passes by, minding its own business, not causing any harm or trouble. Time wouldn't nudge any one of us to refocus when we are drifting away from the path God has called for our lives. This is the danger of wasted time. If time were loud and irritating, I believe we would pay closer attention to it. But, since time is passive, we don't bother it and it doesn't bother us.

Our work is to be aggressive with the football—dreams, goals, visions, and plans. Wasted time is not our friend. For every one of the moments we have in a given day, we must give it our all, and leave no play on the field. For the chances we let waste away, we have to be mindful and play as if there may not be another shot at the end zone. Let us not put off the passions God is stirring in our hearts. The play clock is ticking.

Time is running out, but the good news is that you and I possess the ball. The enemy knows that if he can win with time he doesn't need to do something spectacular to throw you off your game. What are we waiting on? Let us get out there and make it happen.

This is the game-winning drive. This is our day and now is our time.

I recall years ago being at work on one bright Saturday afternoon, when I leisurely pondered what I would do for the rest of my day. Maybe, I thought to myself, I will just waste the evening doing nothing. It was a beautiful day. Maybe I would take my family out to dinner. I was in no hurry to do anything.

Just as I stood there daydreaming, an older gentleman walked into the store with a small box. It contained a stack of documents. While he spoke with one of my colleagues, I overheard his unique request. He pulled out a wrinkled note, folded in half. He put on his reading glasses and began to read the letter quietly to himself. He had a strange sense of urgency in his eyes. He wanted to ship the box to a jail. For a moment, my colleagues and I stopped and looked at each other. "Did the man just say ship these to jail?" we all must have thought quietly to ourselves at the same time.

The man continued to look closely at the note as he attempted to read the handwriting. It was indeed to be sent to someone who had been incarcerated. He read the inmate's name, number, address, and the first few sentences of the letter. Then he expressed the urgency of the box being delivered as quickly as possible. Someone's life was at stake, to such an extent that he could not wait another moment for the package. We imagined it had to be something very important.

At this point, I walked closer and asked the man exactly what he wanted us to assist with. He explained that he had been working on behalf of a young man in jail, whose case had him jumping through hoops. He had a bewildered expression on his face. It was then I recalled seeing him the previous Saturday. He was sending the documents contained in the box to a friend who was looking to represent himself in an appeal from death row.

The gentleman looked at the letter once more and asked us to do whatever it took to ship the documents. It could not arrive one minute later. It did not matter to him how much it cost to send the letter to the person who was probably eagerly waiting for it; the timing was more important than any price that he would have to pay. Time was of the essence.

A person sitting on death row doesn't have the same time the rest of us have to while away precious moments, and go through life casually. Whatever had caused his life to be confined behind bars, there was nothing more precious than the rest of the time he had on his hands. On one end, he had to confront the reality that he might never see his family and friends ever again. Yet on the other end of the same spectrum, he had to do everything in his power to get a chance to live free, someday. Every new day brought him closer to a day he dreaded. Every wasted second is one that he could never get back, so he had no choice but to live as purposefully as he could.

Unfortunately, the rest of us who have the freedom to do anything we can imagine, seldom take advantage of it. If there is anything to learn from the urgency of the man who now cherishes every second, it would be that there is no time to waste time. The truth remains that the same time that you and I waste without giving it much thought could be the same time someone else desperately needs.

Our Heavenly Father gives us all the same amount of time in a day: 24 hours, 86,400 seconds. We may not have the energy to count every second, but we must make every second count. Everyone who has been pressed for time in an emergency before, knows this, that time is one of the most valuable commodities we all have. It is as precious as it is priceless. Time is divine, we can't control or create more, but we are responsible for managing our God-given time.

Every moment matters, and like a quarterback standing on a field with a swarming defense rushing to unravel our plans, every second is meaningful. Every hour is a privilege Almighty God hands to us, every day is divine, every week is a gem, every month is monumental, and every year is vital. There is a ticking clock that we cannot afford to be staring at aimlessly while life passes us by.

HAVE A HURRY-UP OFFENSE

You and I have been chosen for a time such as this for a
victorious life. God has not called us to be timid and unsure
of what the future holds. Like a quarterback on life's proverbial
football field, we walked onto the field equipped. Even when
there seems to be not enough to get into our huddles, we can be
confident that there already is a play within us.

Whenever we are faced with a scenario to move quickly, we
can lean wholly on the strength of Christ, trusting that "He
who had begun a good work in us, is sure to bring it to a fruitful
end." We have to continue to do the things we already know to
do, and trust the Coach's instruction to lead us. Listening to our
quarterback Coach assures us that we are moving along in the
right direction, and with a purpose.

There is a popular quote, "Don't fear failure." But in that
same vein, let us ask ourselves, "Are we scared of success?" There
is no time to be afraid of getting into the end zone, especially if
we are determined to see our dreams come true.

One of the striking differences between life and a football
game is how the latter makes provision for lost time. Occasionally
the referees will wind back the clock to make up for lost time. In
this game of life, however, there is no time added to the clock.
We have to keep ploughing ahead. We cannot get ahead by just
looking around, especially when God had destined you and me
for greatness.

We have to move forward in every endeavor, because for all
we know, we are closer to the end zone than we think. Satan and
his defense will not be standing back applauding our efforts.
The closer we are to the red zone, the tougher it gets. When our

opponent, the defense, sees us getting closer to the end zone, they would have no choice but to work their hardest to derail us from whatever God has in store for you and me.

Some of us may think that the closer we get, the easier life will become, but we have to understand that pressing forward in the tough moments means there isn't much room for error. The closer we get to our dreams, the more formidable an opponent the defense will seek to become.

We have to make it a priority to get after the things we have been called to do. We have to tell ourselves that we are squeezing every dose out of every day, every ounce out of it every hour, every moment out of every minute, and every second out of every situation. We have to get busy and live life.

We must move at a rapid pace when moving in pursuit of the end zone. This is called a hurry-up offense. It is a strategy every team prepares to execute when they have to move quickly and take advantage of every second. The hurry up offense is a go-all-out, and all hands-on-deck scenario This type of offense requires no huddle.

In the same manner, if we have been accepted into Christ's family through salvation, we should be in a hurry-up offensive mode. There is no time to gather around and socialize in holy huddles. We need to hurry up and progress towards our dreams, goals, and visions, because someone is depending on us to pull it off—for us to score and for us to make it. If we succeed, others will feed off our success. We have to hurry up and get down the field to run the plays that God our Heavenly Coach has designed for us.

We know that Satan is nothing but a thief, and one who comes to seek, kill and destroy (John 10:10). Satan and his squad are not just seeking to do one thing or another, they are looking to ruin everything in us. We must know who the thief is. His name is Lucifer the devil and he is the leader of the already defeateddefense on the other side of the ball. He tries to steal time, kill dreams, and destroy lives. One thing that the defensive opponent, the devil, is fully aware of is the fact that he cannot stop us and our high-powered offense. But as children of God, although we have the lead, we should have a fixed focus as if we are playing from behind. We cannot afford to lose sight of the fact that time is ticking, we're playing on the road, and the crowd is loud. Everyone is chanting against our progress, with a host of distractions, and they are not cheering for you.

The good news is that if we are alive today, we are yards away. In our hearts, we can look down at the sideline and see the coach signaling us to keep moving, and know that He will be just as excited when we make a play and win the game.

We must seize the moment and take advantage of the opportunity that comes across our path. It is a privilege to be able to live and play in the big game of life. This is something that we should not take lightly. We must execute with the time that we have. It is important that we protect the ball and never take our position for granted. We are capable, equipped and trained to win. We must buckle up our chin straps and make the most of our offensive possession. We can walk up the field and play full force with confidence, knowing that we can only win.

Executing God's game plan may not look promising at times, and that is because we have trained ourselves to look at it through our own limited lenses. But the great reassurance starts with finding a way to keep working through the noise because it's crunch time, and there is no other option. It doesn't matter if we have to throw it deep or short, whether we have to pitch it or run it; the only thing that matters is to just keep the drive going while implementing the Coach's game plan. We have the advantage of a God who has never failed, and His perfect record will not change with you and me.

We will have to do our best to embrace every opportunity with the passion and excitement like a committed and fearless player. It is in that moment that we have to stand as the courageous quarterback who understands that he has the benefit of an offense that is not afraid to run at will, and keep the defense on its toes. If we are to live in the path that God is calling out for you and me, Satan and his defense will not be sure of how to defend players like us.

The moment is too precious to be sitting on the sidelines of life complaining. The assignment God is calling us to accomplish is too important for us to walk aimlessly on a field when the opposition is busy plotting its attack. Our work is to have complete faith in the Coach's play call and confidence in the team He has called us to be a part of. The clock is ticking, the seconds are fading, and our Heavenly Father is nudging you and me to go for it. Let us determine to become the difference in the game.

CHAPTER TWELVE

TIME OUT

Grace for the Next Turn

Play Call: Matthew 11:28-29

"Come to me, all you who are weary and burdened, and I will give you rest. Take my yoke upon you and learn from me, for I am gentle and humble in heart, and you will find rest for your souls."

Our model for excellence is Jesus Christ, who when He had done all he could in a day, knew to retreat and recharge. Jesus knew in order to continue to pour into the lives of the people he had to take timeout to commune with the God the father—our Head Coach. The life we live is a long-distance journey, and one that we cannot expect to breeze through in a split second.

Sometimes in the game of life, we must take a timeout to recharge and rejuvenate our weary feet. Just as there are both planned and unplanned time-outs that occur in the game, and the coaches know that their quarterbacks need to rush to the sidelines for a moment for water, so should you and I take time to recharge. If we learn to tap into Christ's amazing grace, he will revive our lives into confronting another day with a confidence that we will always be equipped for the journey. *Time out* is not an idle moment.

We can appreciate every moment of play even with the interruptions, because God's hand in our lives never stops working just because we are pausing to recharge. Time-outs are necessary, meaningful, and must be called at the right time. They allow us to review our strategy, and talk to our team of coaches whose perfect love continues to carry us. It is in the timeouts that we are able to rest and retreat to spend a silent and meaningful moment away from life's busy chaos.

In the time out, the moment we do this, we get a moment to rest.

One of the enemy's defensive plays against us is predicated on our fatigue. He knows if he can get us too winded to operate at our best, we will be too worn out to win. If he can't get us winded, he will try to slow us down in every facet of the game, and from there he will try to wear us down. He wants us to become too drained to dream.

Satan and his opposing forces are counting on this tactic to weigh down our mental sharpness, readiness, and ability to make the best decisions that are pleasing to God. Then after, he wants us to become too weak to win or to push through the challenges that the days bring our way to win. He knows if he can get us living at an exhausting pace, , we won't have the strength or power to perform and play to our full potential, and live up to the standard our Heavenly Coach, God our Father, has called us to play.

Time outs give us the opportunity to assess where we are on the field, and retool where we need to. We get the perfect chance to examine which plays are effective and what else we need to do differently to win the game.

One thing that is perhaps undeniable is the fact that, just as the football game many people in North America spend much of their Sundays watching, life is just as rough a sport. We cannot make any headway running on empty. We need the stamina, and above all, the mindset that we are in it to win. We are committed and dedicated to going all the way, and playing the complete game. For whatever purpose God had set us apart, our passion should be to set our minds on living our full potential to bring Him the glory. We are going the full length of the field, and one that is laden with many obstacles, but we count on our Coach's unfailing love. We are not shaken.

It is better to make provision for a time out, than to be in a situation where life's events force us to take a time out because we run out of energy for the battle we wage against an enemy who seeks any sliver of advantage to strike. We should not let an injury, sickness, the loss of a loved one, or a job force us to take a time out. When we take the necessary time outs that allow us to re-focus and adjust, we will be able to handle the distractions and continue playing the game.

We can't afford to get so wrapped up in the game, in life, that we forget to use our time outs when we need to use them. One thing is for sure, a time out is not useful at the end of the game. There aren't any prizes, rewards, metals, or trophies given for possessing all our time outs, and running through life weary and exhausted.

I remember one of the most important pieces of advice my dad gave to me: time cures everything. My dad was absent many years during my youth, as he served time in Leavenworth penitentiary in Kansas. By the time he was released, I was in my twenties and past some of the most formative and instrumental years of my life. He couldn't get back the lost years. This he knew and he was determined to make every effort to spend quality time with me and my siblings. The enemy had meant this to be a dark cloud in his life, yet through this God used him to become a remarkable reflection of a fulfilling life, one that was to leave a legacy of honor and dignity. There was nothing more important to my dad than spending time with me. Incarceration helped him understand the value and importance of time. He was now dedicated to devoting his time to whoever needs a helping hand, and very much fashioning his own life in a Christ-like manner. He knew the value of the simple moments, and making sure he spends life's more precious hours—every opportunity he had—genuinely ensuring others he knew were doing well.

He remembers how he once hurried through life, not stopping for a moment to evaluate the step he was taking. If he had to do it all again, he would make sure his intermission moments were meaningful and well spent. During life's time-outs, we all make small adjustments, strategize, and get back onto the field with a renewed zeal to win the game. In situations where we feel our backs are up against a wall, we cannot panic. But that may very well be the moment we retreat into a quiet rest in the shadow of the Almighty who knows everything we will need even before we ask. When it is necessary, we take the time-out and get ready to relaunch.

PEP TALK

There comes a time in the game when we might have to give ourselves a pep talk. We may have to encourage ourselves, get ourselves fired up, and motivated. We can do this because we have a God on our side who knows all of our shortcomings and till is committed to take us higher. Jesus Christ laid down his life to save you and me, and moreover sent the Holy Spirit to accompany us in every step we take. He guides us along the path to victory, and leads us in the way of winning. When the road seems confusing and the journey seems overwhelming, that is when we stand on the word of God that reassures us, and tell ourselves that we can persevere. You are great! It's not over!

When we step away for a time out to recharge, that is when we get to look in the mirror point to ourselves, and say, *"I Woke Up 2 Win."* We are winning because we woke up. We are forever changed with the DNA of Almighty God woven into every one of us. The best is yet to come because we have the best Coach in the world guiding our steps. You and I are the greatest assets on our teams, and there is a world counting on us to be the salt and light that reflects God's grace. We need to dig our cleats in, and remember that we are a part of a team that wins. When we are on the field we are a threat to the enemy.

We must be alert and know when to say "yes" and "no." We cannot afford to sweat the small things that are inconsequential in the grand scheme of things. Since we know that there is a time and place for everything, our focus should remain on the big picture.

In our daily walk, we must have a strong mind because there will be a lot of things happening on the field to derail us from the game plan. It is through our latching on to every promise and word of our Head Coach that we equip ourselves and show mental toughness.

Don't panic when you're winning, have complete confidence when walking on life's field, with the mindset and attitude to dominate. Appreciate every great play knowing that the opponent will not join in the celebration because you are winning. You are the champion and every moment is a championship moment. Handle the pressure and tune out the crowd noise. Don't worry if fans are not cheering you on.

There is a grace for the next challenge ahead, and if we are running on full power, we are able to exploit the defense by remaining focused. We can never allow Satan's schemes to dim our light. The opposition does not want us to shine. When we are winning, the defense will work their hardest to overturn every single hope of glory God has embedded in our lives, by attempting to plant seeds of doubt in our hearts.

When we are winners, our actions speak for themselves. We will not have to tout our credentials; rather we have to show up in a confidence that is rooted in the blood of Jesus Christ. Winning is normal for us, so we have to expect to win. The challenge for us will be to stay cool even when things get heated. It is during the pep talk that we reaffirm the promise on which we stand, and allow God's word to seep into our subconscious mind.

Our confession of faith and declaration should be,

I win by having no fear,
I win by holding my head up high,

I know nothing else but winning,
Winning is in my blood,
Victory is in my veins,
I'm winning from head to toe,
I won't even give the opposition a chance,
I wake up with the mentality that I've won,
I go to bed with the mentality of a winner.

When we have done all we can, and feel for a moment that we cannot push any further, perhaps the best thing for us to do is to still manage to stand. Just stand, instead of giving up and sitting on the proverbial field when there is a game still left to be played, and a victory still ahead.

Some of the greatest quarterbacks who became famous in football all had an uncanny ability to remain calm while pressed on all sides by the opposing team, the defense. They had learned the art of taking a moment to breathe, reminding themselves of a skill they had mastered long before the defense swarmed around them.

Likewise, we hear of some of the greatest people of our generation having to endure tremendous adversity. What separated them from the millions of others whose stories we never heard, was the simple fact that they stood tall when they had every reason to crumble in defeat.

One of the most important jobs of a quarterback—and for each of us at the helm of our own lives—is the ability to understand the magnitude of the task at hand. This skill takes a lot of preparation through studying our coach's playbook and taking the time to watch the game film, the replay of the moment passed that we can learn from and grow.

When situations seem as if they are spiraling out of control, and when it looks like the four walls are closing in, God is counting on you and me to fight against our natural human instinct to give in, and remain calm and fearless. Our ability to make the right decisions with precise accuracy is the key to converting through tough circumstances. It is in those moments that whatever training we have done will come to our rescue.

Sometimes, to escape the pressure, we will need to take a few steps up, all the while, trusting that God's will for our lives would never lead us into shame, but instead will charge us to keep standing. This will take faith, trust, courage, and mental toughness rooted in whose we are, not who we are. The quarterback that we become shows poise in the pocket in the face of the oppressor, not because of our own skill, but because of who leads us.

We take a time out, surrendering our will to that of Almighty God who assures the tired and the weary to find rest in Him. In the mighty storms of life, our Coach's voice in our helmets reminds you and me to not let the defensive ploys of Satan block our vision from seeing the field clearly. The good news is that the devil knows nothing about our future, so he is powerless against what God has called us to become.

What Satan reviews is our history, and he studies past tendencies. He strategizes through the five senses of the flesh, seeing, hearing, smelling, tasting, and touching. The corrupted coach uses these things that tend to draw our physical attention as points of attack to expose us. He likes nothing more than to replay and rehearse our previous game tapes, our past over and again.

When we are worn out and not at our best is when Satan jumps at the most inopportune times in order to control our future actions. We can choose to hold on to the declaration that we are more than conquerors. Satan does not want us to spend time with God our Coach, or go into the film room. He knows also that spending time in the presence of our Coach is how we learn about his schemes and make the proper adjustments to launch into our victory.

When we feel our hearts fainting in the face of challenges and it is hard to fight on, we ought to unwaveringly examine our thought life. We cannot afford to spike the ball or give in if there is still time on the clock. We have a heavenly Coach who is always urging you and me to overcome Satan's suggestions and reject the tempting thoughts of giving up on the play. Thoughts produce momentum. Thoughts when we are at our lowest points, and drained by a day's pressure can cause a negative momentum and set us up for a mental slump.

One of the greatest assets we have is the people God places in our lives. In Genesis 2:18, God said, "It is not good for the man to be alone. I will make a helper suitable for him." For some of us fortunate to have the company of a wife, we cannot miss the fact that not only does she know the game, she is right on the field playing the game as well.

In Honor of Lindell Broden
Rest in Jesus

CHAPTER THIRTEEN

FOURTH QUARTER

THE URGENCY OF NOW

WHEN YESTERDAY IS TODAY, AND TOMORROW IS NOW

Play call: John 9:4

---

*"As long as it is day, we must do the works of him who sent
me. Night is coming, when no one can work."*

Just because it is fourth quarter does not mean that the game is over. Our lives do not come to a standstill simply because we walk into a season that seems to be all over. Maybe walking into that chapter of our lives demands that we move faster, and run with a sense of urgency. It never is a time to discard the hope with which we have carried on through life until this moment. Instead of crisis, what we are given is a chance to be more aggressive about God's plans for us to move the ball down the field quickly to score the game-winning drive.

You and I are quarterbacks in our own teams, and we are spending time walking with our Head Coach and learning through his Word, and his guidance. The Holy Spirit lives with us and nudges us at every turn. We have a voice in our helmets that is telling us to line up into our winning formation and continue marching down the field.

We can allow God lead us to do the improbable, or listen to the voices that yells against us, and give up. Instead of limiting God, let us stretch our faith and run our life's race with determination, knowing that there is nothing, absolutely nothing, that is too difficult for our God to do.

The New England Patriots and the Atlanta Falcons took to the field for a highly anticipated Super Bowl contest. It was a match between two of the best teams, with each having fought a long and hard battle to earn their place at the game.

Each team had been through adversity and overcome it, game after game. They knew what was at stake, and were aware that the players across the field from them wanted all the glory and much as they did. Neither of the teams could waste the opportunity, and neither could afford to let the opponent gain an advantage.

The Atlanta Falcons began the game flawlessly, doing everything they had to do without missing a heartbeat. All the players were determined to win the game at all costs and there was nothing that would stand in their way. One minute after another, they scored. The Falcons gradually took a lead that destined them for glory. The team has managed to gain such a sizeable lead that even their coaches and team owners walked down to the sideline to join in jubilation. The game was still ongoing, but the Falcons were convinced that there was probably no way the Patriots could overcome this seemingly insurmountable lead.

The competition moved into the fourth quarter. This would become the final moment when they would secure their victory. What the Atlanta Falcons had never anticipated was the fact that despite an opposition that seemed to have everything gone wrong for them throughout the entire game, the Patriots had not given up. Not yet.

The Patriots knew this, that although they had gone onto a field and failed to play to their potential, they could turn that around and stretch themselves to live up to their potential. They could exceed it and believe in something they never thought was possible. The Patriots players knew exactly what they were made up of and they knew what they had endured to get to that field. None of the long days of preparation had been a waste. They remembered the seemingly unsurmountable odds they'd had to overcome along the way, and they knew there was a power within them to do the improbable. The commentators showed statistics of an unlikely scenario. The Patriots were confronted with something no team had ever done, and the curtain was supposedly closing in on their victory. It had to be over.

The Patriots didn't think it was over. They didn't accept the idea that the lead they had surrendered to their opponents through the first three quarters had sealed their fate. The game wasn't over. They had been champions before, and there was a coaching staff on the sidelines reminding them that they would be champions again. They believed the unthinkable, when the rest of the world was staring at statistics that spelled their doom. They chose to believe in the unlikely scenario even when it seemed the opposing team had already begun their victory party. It was now the fourth quarter. It was go-time. It was the moment to step out and snatch a victory that had been theirs all along.

The New England Patriots knew something profoundly simple. They knew whose they were. It didn't matter who they were, as long as they knew whose they were. They knew the DNA that ran through them that called them world changers, overcomers and winners. And they knew who stood on the sidelines as their head coach. They had a coach and a staff who didn't flinch when it seemed like their dreams were sinking, and their confidence didn't wane when the statistics appeared on the giant screens to tell them it was over. They chose to tune out the noise and turn their eyes away from the celebration across the field. They knew they still had work to do. It was the fourth quarter and there was a game on the line.

The Patriots had a quarterback who had grown to believe in his coach's every word. The quarterback, like you and me, had taken the time to study the playbook with his head coach and he knew that no matter how bleak the moments got, there was nothing too difficult for his coach to overcome. The quarterback believed. It was the fourth quarter, and the crowd seemed to be cheering louder for the opposing team.

The Patriots quarterback listened closely to the words of his head coach and started marching his team down the field. One play after another, they began what would become one of the more improbable comeback victories in history. It was one simple pass after another. It was one heroic moment after another. It was one pep talk after another. When they seemed to have every reason to give in and give up, they chose to lay aside the weight that would have kept their focus away from the prize. When they almost didn't have a reason to, they chose to persevere.

The fourth quarter becomes tense for a team that is doing all they can to win. The team that is already leading wants to do everything they can to maintain a steady pace and use as much time as possible. They want to "milk the clock" and waste precious moments. On the other side of the ball is the trailing team and time is extremely crucial for them. This is when they have to open the playbook and execute their best options. This is their time to show what they're made of.

They will execute what they rehearsed in practice, and in this crucial quarter, there's no time to hold back. We are putting everything we are on the line because now is the time to win.

How we respond in the fourth quarter makes all the difference in the world. It can either complement our game or discredit the first three quarters as being a waste of our time. We will have to make the tough decisions we didn't necessarily have to make in the previous quarters. Maybe not every play, pass, and point will come to us as easily in the fourth quarter because we are always engaged in battle with Satan and his defense who fight their hardest to ensure that our lives do not bring our Heavenly Coach the glory. The defense knows that time is running out. We must continue our pursuit to the end zone in order to fulfill our victory and seal our win.

It is the fourth quarter in our own lives, with every moment so precious. We know too that there is a God who is in the business of taking our ashes of failure, rejection and pain, and exchanging them for beauty. There is a God who is our own Heavenly Father who specializes in the impossible.

Our heavenly Head Coach specializes in unlikely come-backs, and He is the one who has gone to extraordinary lengths to draft you and me. God knew before the foundations of the earth that there would be a day when we would have to launch the greatest comeback in our own lives, and He prepared each of us for the moment. Our Coach's unblemished record is at stake through all of our lives, and He is not about to fail. The work left to you and me is to lay aside the weight, and run our race, solely fixing our gaze on the author of our faith.

THE TWO-MINUTE WARNING

The two-minute warning in a football game is important because it signifies that the game is nearing its end. It is the moment in time where we will see how far our work over the first 58 minutes has brought us. There is still a game to be played, and we have to be disciplined to focus on the task at hand. The decisions we made on previous plays have already happened and there is nothing we can do to change them. What will not be productive is if we spend too much time thinking about what could have been and should have been. Our focus should be on the next play.

God warns us and gives us time to make the proper adjustments to fix our game. His grace and mercy is everlasting, and he is patient; but it will be in our own interest to not take the warnings for granted.

If we paid more attention to the referees' penalty flags and learn from these mistakes we could position ourselves for the opportunity to make a play on the game-winning drive and keep the winning streak alive.

The fourth quarter isn't the moment to rest on our achievements, but to run hard with the football. This is when our coaches are calling us to run with intensity, purpose, passion and be mindful of the game-clock. Remember three things: we're on offense, we have the ball, and that the game-clock is running down. There is no time to have regrets about the game we have played; however, it is time to correct anything that was not properly executed. The critical task at hand is to run God's offense as he has instructed us to do, finish strong and win the game.

Our lives remain in the hands of an Almighty God who knows everything and sees everything. He is asking you and me to lean wholly on Him, especially in the crunch time moments when we cannot afford a missed opportunity, and when we're on the verge of achieving what He has called us to become. We have to want to win. The truth is that we are too close to our end zone to run trick-plays. We have to stick with what has been proven to work and run the plays that put us in the best position to score in the first place. God's promises are a sure foundation, and it never changes. His word is powerful and alive, and trusting His guidance will bring us to the expected end.

How would we play the game if we knew we were going to win? Would we go for more shots down the field, play a little looser, have a little more fun, and laugh a little louder? There comes a time that you must GO FOR IT! Go for your dreams. Go for your vision. Go for things God has prepared for you and me to fulfill our destiny. We must play every moment in this game of life like Jesus is watching because He is indeed watching, and cheering us on. We know that our Heavenly Coach is counting on you and me to make the tough plays, the wise decisions, and to be smart with the football. We have come too far to fumble the promise God has birthed inside of each of us. Our coach knows what we are capable of, so we can be confident and play without any timidity—play to win.

Winning is not always easy, and we go through life aware of this reality. There will be many long nights and early mornings when we have to find strength within ourselves to get up and keep moving. There will be times where our resources will not match the needs we have to meet, and the only consolation will have to be standing on God's word that "He shall supply all our needs according to His riches."

We cannot allow the hurdles that cross our path to deter us or entice us to throw the ball away. There will come a time, if we are fearless and go for it, that there will be a reward worth the journey, once you leap over them. Like the quarterback who understands the magnitude of the final quarter, and knows that he is close to achieving his goals, dig your cleats in deep and grind it out.

We thank God for His grace and mercy because He allows us the opportunity to go for it. While we are in the pursuit of moving the ball of our dreams and visions, we must take some risks. There is no time to be passive and shy about moving the ball. Now is the time to make it happen.

When yesterday becomes today, and tomorrow becomes Now.

CHAPTER FOURTEEN

TOUCHDOWN

VICTORY... TO GOD BE THE GLORY

Play Call: Revelation 12:11

"They overcame him with the blood of the Lamb and the testimony of the saints."

Touchdown! Standing above what we set out to accomplish, we can look back and breathe a sigh of relief that we reached our goal, through thick and thin. The touchdown symbolizes everything the football player desperately wants and hopes for in the game. It is what the endless grind of the game is all about and why it's played. In a football game, the touchdown is the emphatic declaration of triumph. It demonstrates victory, power and domination.

Reaching the end zone is the goal we have worked hard for, studied life's perplexing moments, and trained for. The moment we cross the goal line and see the officiating referee raise both hands signaling a touchdown, we will have walked into a promise that has been ours since the foundations of the earth.

There was once a time when the Heavenly Father who loves you and me so much, called us by name, and set us apart for His glory. There was a time when God scouted us patiently even when we were unworthy, and drafted us into his perfect team. Winning is our destination and a touchdown is our pronouncement that we have walked the path that our Coach intended for us, to ultimately bring Him the glory through the life we live. We acknowledge that scoring points is a difficult challenge, but we remember also that we suited up for life and there was no turning back. It was for this reason that we were selected, so that the will of God would be made evident in this life. You and I are called for a purpose, and God is looking for an opportunity to display his handiwork through every one of our lives.

The touchdown is where we get to stand back, even for a split moment, without any regrets because we have made it to any height we set up to reach. Just as in a football game, it would matter very little what a player had to endure to cross the plane into the end zone. In the celebration of what God has called us to do, we know how every step and stride, and every pain and tear, had been for a purpose. We have made it, and that is what counts the most.

To cross the threshold for a touchdown we would have given the journey our maximum effort and forged ahead even when it seemed like we had exhausted all our strength to move another step. For every accomplishment, we would have made it into the proverbial end zone through a determination day after day. We would have had to walk through the rain and pushed harder through the beating sun with a no-matter-what-it-takes attitude and a stick-with-it-ness because we saw a target ahead, and had the advantage of a Head Coach who has our best intentions at heart guiding us every step along the way.

Our struggle to the end zone has been to bring God Almighty the glory that he takes from you and me, as fallible as we are, and turns our lives around into something wonderful. Our touchdowns are the evidence that if we are able to leave our hearts and desires in the hands of our Head Coach, He has all the power to take us to heights we never could have reached on our own.

Sure, we sometimes have to high-step to get into the end zone, and sometimes we might have to run in with full force, jog in, jump in, fall in, or even crawl in. The "how" really doesn't matter; God is calling you and me to just find our way into the end zone.

A win is a win, and every yard and inch it takes to get there is a reminder that regardless of our shortcomings when we were drafted, there was an incredible assignment ahead for us to accomplish. We couldn't take anything for granted. All the sweat, blood, and battle bruises were for a bigger purpose. Indeed it is in standing at the end zone that we get to see that there was no value in comparing the blessings and benefits that the touchdown represents.

The thrill of a touchdown wouldn't pack the exciting punch that it embodies without battle wounds and accrued scars. In the game of life there will always be injured players who would do anything to get back on a team's active roster to have another chance to get on the field. It is by grace that you and I get the chance to forge ahead through even in the most difficult moments, get to be on the field, and be part of the action. We push our way into the end zone because we know that God has not called us to sit on the sidelines and watch the time pass us by.

A touchdown is worthy of a team's celebration. We have been fortunate to have our teammates contributing to the plays that led to the end zone. In doing so, they helped us reach our calling and purpose.

Our lives are vessels through which God's magnificence is shown to the world. Once the game is over, just as the player wants to hear the words "great game" from their coach, we have a Coach who cheers us on at every turn and has full confidence in us. Affirmation from Him makes the victory that much sweeter, and it is in pleasing Him with our work and hearts that we continue to represent His perfect team. God is calling you and me to continue to suit up, step on the field, roll up our sleeves, and go to work.

Coaches spend many hours pouring their hearts into teaching, mentoring, leading and guiding players. They dedicate their time, expertise, and skillset to their players. It means so much when they confirm that a great game was played. In fact that was the image of excellence He saw in you and me when he fearlessly and masterfully breathed life into us.

Celebrating the moment of a touchdown is recognition of the process and the grind. The victory is well worth the hardships that come with scoring. Our winning touches the lives of many more people than our own. I think about all the people who celebrate a touchdown in a football game: the fans, the cheerleaders and even the mascot. The cheerleaders, coaches and teammates cherish every stride we take. They all feel the impact of the touchdown because someone decided to gear up as a spiritual athlete to fight toward whatever God has called him or her to do. There is the celebration because you and I decided to buckle our belt of truth, put on the shoulder pads of righteousness, and come into the game ready to run with the gospel of peace. We know that to play in this game we must shield ourselves with faith, and ensure that our heads are pro-tected with the helmet of salvation, because we have been called to bring God the glory. We have been called with a mandate to *Wake Up to Win.*

The words from Ephesians 6:10-17 is a glaring reminder that we have all that it takes to excel in the journey. "Finally, be strong in the Lord and in his mighty power. Put on the full armor of God, so that you can take your stand against the devil's schemes. For our struggle is not against flesh and blood, but against the rulers, against the authorities, against the powers of this dark world and against the spiritual forces of evil in the heavenly realms. Therefore, put on the full armor of God, so that when the day of evil comes, you may be able to stand your ground, and after you have done everything, to stand."

The chapter goes on to reiterate the need to keep our focus on the assignment even when it doesn't seem that our own might is good enough to push us over the line. The caution is to "Stand firm then, with the belt of truth buckled around your waist, with the breastplate of righteousness in place, and with your feet fitted with the readiness that comes from the gospel of peace. In addition to all this, take up the shield of faith, with which you can extinguish all the flaming arrows of the evil one.

Take the helmet of salvation and the sword of the Spirit, which is the word of God."

Nothing in our life has been a waste. It is after we have made that game-winning drive, that most of us can appreciate being able to make it up the field of life. We may have not appreciated the time spent on the 20-yard line when we still were working our way through the path that God is nudging us to follow. At times, the field might have looked long and we weren't sure we could take the opportunity ahead. In the end, we can remember the fourth-and-inches play when we almost gave up on ourselves after we had come so close to our win, and didn't know.

We persevered because it was all a part of the great game that we live to play. Our success was a part of our Coach's game plan, and He loves you and me too much to let us fall apart. We were fortunate, because beyond the magnitude we deserve to have the Blood on our side. Jesus Christ's blood shed for our sake on Calvary is our block, and our perfect hedge of protection.

In Psalmist wrote, "For the Lord God is a sun and shield: the Lord will give grace and glory: no good thing will he withhold from them that walk uprightly"(Psalm 84:11). There is no quarterback who has ever been successful without his blockers helping him get the ball past the tough aggressive defenders and the oncoming speedy pass-rushers.

God gives most of us the benefit of a good wife or husband, one whose role is to be our helpmate, teammate, cheerleader, and ultimately stand along us as the Most Valuable Player (MVP) of the game. The wife or the husband makes personal sacrifices for the team and it is important to understand that he or she is a key component to the offense that has you and me at quarterback. Our work, every step along the way, is to reaffirm their value in our lives, because they help us gain yards and move the chains on the field of life.

We run our race through life as quarterbacks destined for victory, and our task is to make sure that we relay the coach's instructions to our team, especially to the wife or husband who has made the commitment to go through life's trenches with us. They too, celebrate our touchdowns, just as much as they endure our low moments. They are an integral part of the offense, and it is crucial that we understand their strengths.

For the life of the believer, scripture reminds us in John 14:15-17 that the Holy Spirit is in us and that God is for us. Christ cleared the path as our block, protecting us from all the tactics and schemes of the enemy. (Hebrews 9:24.) This is part of the promise and covenant that we have with God the Son, and that is what guarantees our *touchdown*.

PRAYER IS OUR OFFENSIVE LINE

Prayer packs a powerful punch. Prayer is to us as shrink-wrap is to a pallet. Although it seems thin, a surprisingly small amount of it can hold tons of material together. Every spiritual athlete—striving for every yard, and for the ultimate goal of crossing the line into his dream and aspirations—should recognize the need for prayer. Prayer is our protection, and it is the offensive line that works two-fold: it helps the offense move the ball up the field and it stands guard against the defense.

I have come to find that having prayer as our offensive line is a great part of the game. It opens up opportunities to make big plays and unleashes the power that is in us through Christ's salvation to help you and me get to our ultimate goals. It is ours to use, exists for us to communicate regularly with our coach and the rest of the team.

The comforting truth is that even in the grimmest of moments, we can be assured of the fact that we had been fighting a defeated opponent. Our battle was against Satan who is a pretender and not a contender. His schemes and tactics are a sham, and approach us from all angles, through fear, loneliness, poverty, depression, low self-esteem, and a host of turmoil.

"Likewise the Spirit also helps in our weaknesses. For we do not know what we should pray for as we ought, but the Spirit Himself makes intercession for us. Now He who searches the hearts knows what the mind of the Spirit is, because He makes intercession for the saints according to the will of God." (Romans 8:26-27.)

We can trust that there is nothing we need to make it into the end zone that surprises our Head Coach. We may not know every scripture or play call by memory but as we keep studying the playbook and listening to the coach, there is not a moment that we would be stuck in the dark with no hope in sight. For the assignment for which we have been called, winning demands our getting on our knees and praying. It would not have been about the chatter—the technical mumbo-jumbo—but leaning on our playbook to stay on communication with our Head Coach.

IT'S FIXED. WE WON!

We have a Head Coach whose name is victory. We have a powerful team flanking us on both sides to guarantee that we arrive at the destination that God in His perfect plan desires for each of us. Everything we set our hearts to accomplish, surrendered to the will of Almighty God, comes to fruition because we have a support system on our side that defeated Satan long before we even took the field.

The game was won on the cross while our Savior traded His righteousness for our sins, so that everything we hope to become would come alive, and ultimately bring Him the glory. We get to declare victory, having walked through and fought through the game that God gave us the day he drafted us. "And they overcame him by the blood of the Lamb and by the word of their testimony; and they loved not their lives unto the death" (Revelation 12:11).

We have a coach who desperately wants us to win, but we also must want to win. The caution for you and me is to refrain from working against the system that has been set up for us to win since the beginning. The Lord has fixed the game for us to win in the end, if only we are obedient to walk in the path and in the light of Almighty God. God can use any one of us, and in fact He continues to use the ones that society shunned and underestimated, because in the end, His glory is what will be made manifest. God is still in the business of using "the foolish things of the world to confuse the wise" (1 Corinthians 1:27).

Just as we remember the stories of Moses standing up against the powerful Pharaoh, and David's offense against the enormous giant Goliath, there is no target so distant that God's outstretched arms cannot reach it. There is nothing in the way of our path to the end zone that is competition for God the Father and His game plan. He is undefeated and has a perfect winning record. God, in his infinite wisdom, knows what He is doing. To God be the glory, forever and ever, Amen.

Ultimately, we are not playing the game that the world is playing. Our game plan is different from the already-defeated defense. The manner that we win is different from the corrupted coach approach. We are playing for the ultimate trophy, the crown of life.

And when we reach that end zone we will celebrate the ultimate touchdown, the prize, and the goal. That is when we hear our heavenly coach say, "Well done, my good and faithful servant." You Woke to Win the Big Game of Life.

THE WINNER'S PRAYER™

———

Lord, Jesus, help me on the field today, help me to command the offense and take control on every play.

Help me listen wisely to your play call and follow it according to your plan.

Help me to play unselfishly today; please help me to keep my teammates in mind.

Thank you for allowing me to read the defense and to communicate effectively with my team. Thank you for allowing me to see the blitz of the oppressor from every angle and stand firm making precise, accurate and timely throws. Thank you, Father, for your guidance and protection keeping me upright on every side, not allowing me to buckle, fold, or succumb to pressure.

Thank you for giving me the courage not to be moved or rattled. I thank you, Father, for giving me the strength to stand tall and strong, having complete poise in the pocket.

Lord, I thank you for every possession you allow me to have. Lord, I thank you for every yard you allow me to gain, even the hard ones.

Father, I thank you for every inch, for every conversion, especially on fourth down. Lord, thank you for helping me successfully move the chains.

I thank you, Father, for every point, every touchdown, and every win.

In Jesus' name, amen.

INDEX

REFERENCES

Allen, James, (1903) *As a Man Thinketh*

Beavis ,Wes, (2004) *Give your Life a Success Makeover*

Bridges, Kynan, (2016) *The Power of Prophetic Prayer, Release your Destiny*

Edmonds, E. Obeng-Amoako, (2016)*A Poke in My Eye, When Hope is our only Excuse to Live Again*

Fine, Debra, (2005) *The Power of Meeting People, Start Conversations, Keep them going, Build Rapport, Develop Friendships, and Expand Business*

Hemphill, Ken (2002) *The Prayer of Jesus Journal, An Everyday Adventure with the Father*

Hill, Napoleon, (1960) *Think and Grow Rich*

Giblin, Les, (2001) *The Art of Dealing with People*

Jakes, T.D., (2014) *Instinct, The Power to Unleash your Inborn Drive*

Jakes, T.D., (1997) *So You Call Yourself a Man*

Johnson,Vic, (2003) *Day by Day with James Allen*

Kyne, Peter (2003) *The Story that Tells You How to Become One*

Thieme, R.B. Jr., (1973) *Old Sin Nature vs. Holy Spirit*

THE FIELD OF LIFE

ENDZONE

BJ   FJ   SJ

HATRED
✗

U

ORGIES
AND THE LIKE   WITCHCRAFT
✗   ✗

SELF AMBITION   FACTIONS   ENVY   JEALOUSY   DISCORD   DISSENSION
✗   ✗   ✗   ✗   ✗   ✗

IDOLATRY   DEBAUCHERY   IMPURITY   SEXUAL   DRUNKENNESS   FITS OF RAGE
                           IMMORALITY
✗   ✗   ✗   ✗   ✗   ✗

ACTS OF THE FLESH

FRUITS OF THE SPIRIT

LJ   HL
      ⭘   ⭘   ⭘   ⭘
   FAITHFULNESS   SELF-CONTROL   PATIENCE   KINDNESS

GOODNESS   GENTLENESS
      ⭘   ⭘
        ⭘   ☆   ⭘
     PEACE   QUARTERBACK   JOY
              ⭘
             LOVE

R

ENDZONE

HOME-O

THE DEFENSE
SATAN, DEMONS, PRINCIPALITIES & RULERS OF DARKNESS

THE OFFENSE
GOD, JESUS AND THE HOLY SPIRIT

AWAY-7

WINNING SCHEDULE

What Defensive Opponent Are You Facing Today?

We live our lives in quarters and seasons. As players on the field of life, we face tough opponents every day. Our first step to winning is recognizing that there are things in life that the enemy uses to work against us *(the Acts of the Flesh)*. We must also know that God has equipped us with weapons to win against any defensive opponent *(the Fruits of the Spirit)*.

When executing our life's purpose through the Fruits of the Spirit, we gain yards and succeed on the field of life. We win the Ultimate Game. The objective of the winning schedule is to help us grow and gain yards each time we overcome a defensive opponent. With Christ you **Win**, he will help you with the **Struggles**, and learn from the **Lessons**.

SCOREBOARD

Day - 1 Monday	vs	_____	Wins	Struggles	Lessons
Day - 2 Tuesday	vs	_____	Wins	Struggles	Lessons
Day - 3 Wednesday	vs	_____	Wins	Struggles	Lessons
Day - 4 Thursday	vs	_____	Wins	Struggles	Lessons
Day - 5 Friday	vs	_____	Wins	Struggles	Lessons
Day - 6 Saturday	vs	_____	Wins	Struggles	Lessons
Day -7 Sunday	vs	_____	Wins	Struggles	Lessons

CPSIA information can be obtained
at www.ICGtesting.com
Printed in the USA
FFOW03n1217140518
46643991-48720FF